From the
Fo'c's'le

From the
Fo'c's'le

DAVID KASANOF

SHERIDAN HOUSE

First published 1997 by
Sheridan House Inc.
145 Palisade Street
Dobbs Ferry, NY 10522

The chapters in this book appeared previously in
the "Fo'c's'le" column in *WoodenBoat* Magazine

Selected and edited by Matthew P. Murphy

Publisher's warning: The illustration on the front cover is not
meant to be instructional; rather, it reflects the author's occasional
worldview, as evidenced in some of the following chapters.

Library of Congress Cataloging-in-Publication Data

Kasanof, David, 1931–
    From the fo'c's'le / David Kasanof.
      p. cm.
    "The chapters in this book appeared previously in . . .
WoodenBoat magazine"—T.p. verso.
   ISBN 1-57409-034-8 (alk. paper)
   1. Sailing.   2. Sailboat living.   3. Boats and boating.
I. Title.
GV811.K33   1997
797.1'24—dc21   97-37860
                                        CIP

Designed by Jeremiah B. Lighter

Printed in the United States of America

ISBN   1-57409-034-8

C O N T E N T S

Foreword

IT IS FLATTERING to be told by a real live publisher who is not a relative that he thinks that many people would pay to read one's past *Fo'c's'les*, even people who had read them once before. However, selecting the columns to be included seemed to me like asking Mother Hubbard to select her favorite children. So daunting seemed the task, in fact, that I didn't do it (but more of that anon).

The trouble is that they are *all* my favorites, the one I happen to be working on especially. I whoop and guffaw as I write. I'm my own best audience. You'd think that with all that whooping and guffawing I'd be having fun. You'd be wrong. Between whoops and guffaws there lie interminable periods of rocking back and forth. I'm not talking looking at the sunset rocking; I'm talking about clenched teeth rocking. The gestation of a *Fo'c's'le* column resembles the birth of a large mammal more than it does any creative act. (Yeah, yeah, giving birth is a creative act of sorts but so is gaining weight.) If I could produce these columns by Caesarean section while under heavy sedation I'd do it.

Not only do I respond like any reader while writing but so lousy is my memory that months later, when re-reading what I have written when it is printed in *WoodenBoat*, I break up again, having completely forgotten what I wrote. Yogi Berra's wonderful, "It's déjà vu all over again," has no bearing here. I have no recollection of the first vu.

So, in order for me to select columns for this anthology I would have had to re-read every word of every one. There would have been no triggering of the memory after the first sentence or two, after which the entire column would roil to the surface.

That's why Lothar Simon kindly allowed me to beg off making the choices and assigned that enviable task to *WoodenBoat*'s excellent and capable Matt Murphy!

I don't see how he did it; I would have wanted them all to go in, of course. That's especially true of the one I'm currently working on but, alas, you'll have to read it in *WoodenBoat*. I could tell you more about it but I'm laughing too hard.

Introduction

FOR A SUPPOSED old salt I'm a relative newcomer to sailing, having reached my early twenties before setting foot in a sailboat. But when I took the tiller of a friend's sloop it was as if I had been sailing for years. As a child I had been fascinated by the models in New York City's Central Park lake and the hours I had spent watching the models must have taught me a lot about how boats behave under sail. Within an hour of taking the helm I could sail, trim sails, come about and jibe (often intentionally!). Since that time, I have learned little of any additional significance.

Soon my friends and I were given to crossing the Gulf Stream to Bimini in order to participate in various educational and cultural activities offered by that community. On these passages I learned to navigate a little and picked up some valuable cruising tips. For example, after turning down the offers of pilotage by the local entrepreneurs, watch carefully how they return to the harbor entrance. That way, you will know at least where not to go. They routinely go across the shoals in hopes that you try to follow them in. Pulling dumb Americans off the sand is even more lucrative than piloting them in.

Cruising these southern waters, including Biscayne Bay and the Keys, taught me not only how to get big boats off the sand but how to make palatable dinners using the diesel manifold for a hot plate. (Well, maybe not exactly palatable but what the hell, I'm still here.)

I left southern waters to become Associate Editor of the old *Rudder* magazine in New York. During this period I acquired a wife, two large dogs, and a son. We sailed Long Island Sound in a 20-foot *Pennant* class sloop . . . a crowded 20-foot *Pennant* class sloop. The dogs loved to sail and would respond appropriately to the words, "ready about." So would my wife and son but that's not especially noteworthy.

I was the only *Rudder* staffer who owned a boat, so my editor, Conrad Miller, thought it might be a good idea to cover the commissioning of the Larchmont Yacht Club by sailing my little sloop to the event. This I did and arrived in good order in my white topsiders, white ducks, white shirt, and blue jacket with the gold braid *Rudder* logo on the breast pocket. I absolutely refused to wear a yachting cap.

I was directed to a mooring directly in front of the well-populated club veranda. Fearful that I might botch the mooring pickup in front of that critical audience I nevertheless managed to do so without incident. My boat dead in the water, sails all aluff, I walked as slowly as I could to the bow and picked up the pennant eye with studied nonchalance. The launch was about 100 yards away so I had to yell quite loudly for his attention, not having such a civilized device as a horn aboard.

"I'm here for the commissioning of the Yachtmont Larch Club," I bellowed. No one has since taken me seriously.

It was at about this time that Nancy and I started the newsletter *Classic Boat Monthly*. We kept it afloat for a couple of years, putting it together on the dining room table, but with my full-time job it became too heavy a labor. Shortly after I scuttled it I got a call from Jonathan Wilson who was interested in buying my subscribers' list and who wanted me to write a monthly humor column for the new magazine he was starting called *WoodenBoat*. I was flattered to be invited and the rest, as is well known, represents a pinnacle on the topological map of nautical journalism.

Then we found CONTENT lying in Annapolis, bought her, and sailed back to our home in Connecticut. Entering Ambrose Channel under sail on a foggy summer morning I explained to Nancy, who had been dubiously looking at the starboard markers going by on my *port* hand, that I was deliberately sailing down the wrong side of the channel so that I wouldn't be run down by the big ships we could hear but seldom see, hooting through the murk. She shook her head and retired to the galley, intent on breakfast biscuits.

I heard it or rather felt it long before I saw it. A throbbing that means only one thing to a cruising sailor. A great big diesel coming fast. When she got close enough I could see her name, TOYOTA MARU, one of the largest container ships afloat. She was doing 10 knots and dragging half the water in Ambrose Channel with her. That was the first and I hope the last time CONTENT ever took green water over the taffrail. Nancy helped by yelling, "What the hell are you doing?"

To this day I cannot see a Toyota without turning up my collar and ducking my head.

I'm retired now, which means I'm working my rudder loose on

CONTENT, determined to bring her back to the condition she deserves to be in. I know that I have my work cut out for me because every third person who passes me in the yard in Fort Lauderdale says, "You have your work cut out for you." I tell them I expect to be sailing in a couple of years and they laugh, not seeming to take me seriously. They sound like the people at the Yachtmont Larch Club.

PART ONE

Life Aboard
CONTENT

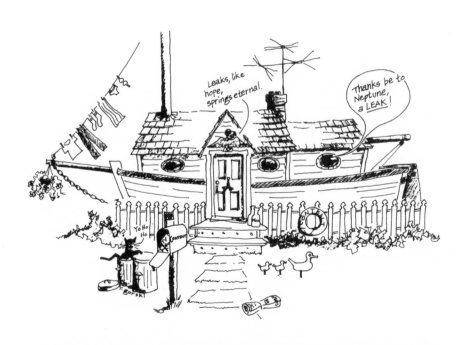

CHAPTER 1

The Fo'c's'le

FOR MORE THAN a couple of reasons, I've always preferred the fo'c's'le for sleeping, reading, or just being alone. Of course, there are some activities that are best accomplished elsewhere in the vessel in order to maintain propriety, but all in all, the fo'c's'le is for me. Perhaps that is because I began my sailing days in big boats as a crewman somewhat lower in the pecking order than the ship's cat and naturally became accustomed to sleeping with my feet in the cabin locker. Perhaps it is because many of my warmest memories are connected with my time in fo'c's'les. I do know that fo'c's'les for me are snug, comfortable, and somehow closer to the heart of the vessel than any other spot.

Try this: Some evening next season, after the dishes are done, the anchor light lit, halyards tied off, and the anchor checked, go into the fo'c's'le, lie down, stay alert, and listen. You can become virtually totally aware of the boat if you do this right. You can hear everything, the faint plip-plip of wavelets striking the hull, the barely audible hiss of an outboard motor perhaps a mile away, amplified by the hull itself. You can perceive the entire boat as an entity, from masthead to keel, in a way that is not quite as vivid as, say, from the main cabin. It's almost as if the boat were a six-inch model and you were viewing it from a vantage point outside the boat. Maybe it has something to do with the fo'c's'le being at one end rather than the middle—but I haven't noticed the same effect from any aft cabins that I've been in. Maybe that's because I've not been invited into enough aft cabins.

I do know that this hyper-aware state in the fo'c's'le has its darker side. There are, when all is said and done, plenty of things I'd just as soon not be middling fair aware of, let alone hyper. Take that "plip-plip of the wavelets on the hull" business. Now, that's just dandy, but let me tell you what once happened to me. I was delivering someone's boat, a Scandinavian double-ender, and had decided to drop the hook for the night in a quiet cove off one of the Florida Keys. As is often the case in these waters, the evening was absolutely calm with the water like glass. I turned in, naturally, in my favorite spot. At about 2 a.m. I awoke to check that everything was secure. It was, and just for fun I remained awake, hyper-awaring it up. Plip plip plip. Long pause. Plip plip plip. Long pause. Plip plip plip, etc. I knew I'd had it. A slight swell had come up—probably straight from hell and, encountering a Scandinavian boat, which was of course lapstraked, produced three distinct plips each time it slapped the bottom edge of a strake. I tried to ignore it, but ignoring something like that once you've heard it is like trying not to think of a white bear. Finally, I had to sing sea chanteys to mask the sound, which after a while began to seem as loud as Niagara. Before morning I had roared out every verse of every chantey I knew several times. I even had to sing "Blow the Man Down," which I detest. At sunrise I was the hoarsest psychotic south of the St. John's River. I suppose that could have happened had I chosen to sleep amidships but the sound certainly seemed more obtrusive in the fo'c's'le.

Fo'c's'les are best for more gregarious activities also. Aren't the impromptu parties, the gams, the bull sessions in the fo'c's'le somehow more fun than anywhere else, especially in foul weather? Stories are funnier, whiskey smoother, and talk far more interesting when, closer to the vessel's skin than you are, say, in the main cabin, you can hear the drumming of rain on the foredeck. Enjoyment of this camaraderie depends, of course, on tight decks. Foredecks don't leak more; it's just that when they do they do it on people. Locating these leaks can be a chore. I know it used to be so for me until I noticed that 94 percent of these leaks were located directly above my left ear. Here's a ship carpenter's tip for correcting such leaks: Observe exactly where the drops strike the cabin sole or bunk. Set your compass for a two-inch radius. Strike a circle around the spot. Don't sit there.

I'll be giving out other helpful hints for the wooden boat sailor from time to time in future gams here in the fo'c's'le.

CHAPTER 2

Getting CONTENT

WELL, SHIPMATES—we've actually done it. A couple of weeks ago we began moving aboard some 25 tons of oak, pitch pine, and bronze in the shape of a 41-foot gaff-rigged English pilot cutter, CONTENT OF FALMOUTH. She's the last boat I intend to buy. Future *Fo'c's'les* will be penned from this 61-year-old hooker with a nearly plumb stem and a bowsprit that I'm afraid to measure. She's a classic beauty and I am just beginning to make her acquaintance.

I have already experienced certain phenomena attendant to owning an old wooden craft that I had not anticipated. Teredos, I had given thought to. Rot, I had worried about. But the owner of a classic wooden vessel must be prepared to contend with a more persistent challenge: public curiosity. On our passage from the Sassafras river at the head of the Chesapeake (where we bought her) to Milford, Connecticut (where we are docked) my abilities as an impromptu lecturer were much more in demand than my seamanship.

The gaff was what intrigued most of them. People in red Bermuda shorts and hats with anchors on them would ask what that other spar was for. Then they would ask about her copper sheathing. Most were intrigued by her obvious physical strength. I found myself repeating the same over and over, from Chesapeake City to Sandy Hook, like a professional tour guide. I think I repeated at least 500 times that her planks are all continuous—no butts. Now, that's impressive, but there aren't many ways to say it. After a while one begins to embellish, just to relieve the monotony.

Even silence once served as embellishment. One Mr. and Mrs. Redshorts, after finding out about the gaff, the sheathing, etc., volunteered, "We understand that you're the folks who are sailing around the world." I saw no need to contradict these good people, so held my tongue. That was in Chesapeake City at the western end of the C and D Canal. The next day in Cape May, at the southern end of the Delaware, total strangers identified us as the intrepid globe-circlers. Still, I kept a humble but dignified silence. Modesty has always been my forte.

Now, at Milford, we are still excavating the previous owner's gear as we settle in. The boat is huge and there was a ship's chandlery aboard. Yesterday, I unearthed a 40-gallon water tank I didn't know about. I'm still trying to find the electric motor that goes "braaak" every time I push a mysterious button in the engine room. I don't know what it does, but it sure runs. Maybe it's a noise maker to keep the putty bugs awake and so drive them away. You can never tell. Those olden timey sailors were pretty smart.

CHAPTER 3

"It's CONTENT!"

AFTER HAVING LIVED aboard old CONTENT OF FALMOUTH for about six weeks, I've realized all too late that the surveyor overlooked the most crucial factor prior to my purchasing her. He didn't survey *me*. The old hooker is sound as a dollar, but what about me? Am I good enough for her? She was built with such inner strength and quality that she comes down to me (after 61 years) in such condition that a bronze nail drawn from her planking a few months ago looks as if it had just come from the chandlery in Falmouth. I, on the other hand, have been known on occasion to lie, procrastinate, boast (even to bend, fold, and mutilate)—generally to give evidence of the tacky nature of my soul. My teeth are full of rare metals and ceramics, my eyes myopic, and I have unbelievably severe dandruff. Any surveyor not in cahoots with the former owner would have thumped my rib cage once and pronounced me hogged, nail-sick, and strained.

Yet, you say, the dear old chap is modest to a fault to admit all this in public. Not so. I admit it only because it is not going to be true much longer. Maybe it isn't even true now. How so? Because the old girl is reforming me. She's working a kind of resurrection. In short, she has challenged me to live up to her. My good seawife, Nancy, already has a stock expression for the phenomenon. When a cheap or easy solution to a problem occurs to me, she'll say, "It's CONTENT!" and I know that I must use bronze screws and not galvanized nails.

The first repair I've completed is the skylight coaming, which had a spot of rot. I cut out the rot and fitted a graving piece, a "dutchman." I've done any number of such repairs on wooden boats I've owned in the past and I know that normally this job would have taken me a weekend, one day to cut and glue, another to plane, sand, and varnish. But, "It's CONTENT!"—I started almost a week ago and the job's not yet done. Ordinarily, I would have part-eyeballed, part-measured the dutchman, cut it, clamped it in place, then sawn down through the sloppy seams once or twice until the seam between the dutchman and the rest of the coaming was good enough to make a strong bond and look OK. Not this time.

"It's CONTENT!" I had in my mind's eye a perfect joint, the kind one sees on fine furniture. So despite the awkwardness of the situation as far as firm clamping was concerned, I set about to achieve perfection. I measured carefully and made the best first saw cut I've ever made. A dockside kibitzer said "perfect" when I test-fitted the newly cut piece. It wasn't good enough. Down through the seam I sawed again. Better, but still not good enough. Again. And so forth, on into the night, working under a light. Finally I got it so that the light from a 100-watt bulb could not be seen through the seam. But there was one trouble. Most of my piece had gone into sawdust. I now had the best-fitting seam of a too-damn-small dutchman any-where north of Macon. I began again. When I finish this writing, I'll finish the sanding and varnishing of the new piece. It's an acceptable fit but it's really not good enough for her. Next time.

You see, I'm beginning to radiate a faint glow of sanctity already and I've hardly been aboard through three spring tides. What will I be like after a few years? My splices will all be served, my bright-work varnished and rubbed, my decks holystoned. I shall emerge shining and spotless, a paragon of seamanlike virtues, well able to live up to this fine vessel, and will probably not speak to any of you at all.

CHAPTER 4

The Principal Hardship

WHAT IS THE principal hardship accruing to those who would, as we do, live aboard year round? Cabin fever? Scurvy? Bubonic plague? Dutch elm disease?—close, to be sure, but all miss the mark. The principal hardship is sympathy, the sympathy—shading into pity—with which people react upon learning that one lives on an old wooden cutter. The tip-off is the way the word "actually" gets inserted into statements. "I understand you are the people who actually live on an old wooden sailboat?" is a typical case. Then come questions indicating some concern for our survival. People want to know if the boat "rocks" or "tilts." Others want to know how and if we keep warm. They give us electric heaters. They festoon us in electric heaters. Ever try tactfully refusing an electric heater proffered by someone convinced that but for his appliance you'd congeal before sundown? It's like trying to refuse a subpoena.

Old CONTENT is so deep (eight feet) that inside her one lives at least half below the waterline and she's so heavily built that her hull serves as an excellent insulator. Consequently, she's very easy to heat. Our main winter heating problem was figuring out where to put all the surplus heaters. With plenty of snow on our decks we kept reasonably snug all winter with one propane heater and an occasionally used electric heater dug from the pile of them aft in the engine room.

Yet, we constantly meet people, even sailors, who can't quite assimilate the fact that we live aboard CONTENT in full accord with her name. Somehow, one can live on a big posh cabin cruiser, or fiberglass "ocean racer-cruiser-weekender" but not aboard an old English cutter, at least not without arousing emotions more appropriate to the contemplation of the plight of the sulphur bottom whale.

Shortly after the winter's ice left the harbor in Milford, Connecticut, we found it necessary to take CONTENT to Stamford, 30 miles west. More than one person asked us, with expressions of great concern, how we were going to effect that move without an engine. If we had owned, say, a Triton I doubt whether anyone would ask, but while people are charmed by CONTENT's *antiqueness*, they often appear surprised that she really does function. It's like finding out that an old pine butter churn, so charming as an umbrella stand, can also make butter.

"Can you sail that thing by yourself?" they ask. (Sometimes, it's "actually sail" in addition to "that thing.")

In fact, CONTENT is quite easy to sail alone in winds below 20 knots. One just does one thing at a time without hurry until the job is done. CONTENT has four running backstays, two topping lifts, and five sheets, all of which must be tended when going about. But in light air, they don't have to be tended quickly. In heavy air, the skipper and his wife must run just as well as the aforementioned rigging. To get in and out of narrow channels when the wind is unfavorable, we lash the dinghy alongside and fire up the three-horsepower British Seagull. Once again, we get curious (sympathetic) stares as we march along at a stately knot and a half. I know they are thinking, "look at those poor devils."

Naturally, when I needed a little sympathy on the passage down Long Island Sound, there was no one around to give it. That was when, in a scant breath of air, running under main, stays'l, and jib (that's all I've got so far), old CONTENT simply stopped. No, not ran aground, but ran out of wind—by Godfrey, stopped. All sails continued to draw but she would not answer the helm. In fact, close inspection of the water surface showed that tidal current was flowing from stern to stem. She was stationary over the bottom with all sails pulling. I rose to the occasion by clenching my teeth and muttering "How can this be, dammit?!" How it could be was by running afoul of a lobster pot buoy is how it could be. After half an hour the bloody thing bobbed to the surface about 10 feet to windward; there was a great boil as CONTENT's expanse of deadwood and keel slid sideways and we slowly got squared off the wind again and underway.

The wind piped up a few hours before we entered through the Stamford breakwaters and we sailed into the outer harbor in fine style, dropped the hook, the main, fired up the Seagull, picked up the hook, and motorsailed down the long channel under both heads'ls. Approaching the dock, I dropped the hook again to use the anchor rode as a springline to stop her. I had a round turn around the bitt and when I thought it was time, I put on the brakes. Nothing happened. Our new home port's bottom mud raised a little cloud as we ploughed along with our 40-pound Danforth. It was like trying to anchor in yogurt. Again, I could have used a little sympathy but there was none available. Those of you who know boatyards don't have to be told that there was no one around to tell us which slip to go to. We picked a spot, tied up, and settled in.

We've begun to make new friends among our neighbor yachtsmen. One of them recently remarked that he was planning to sell his house and live aboard. The poor devil. He has my sympathy.

CHAPTER 5

Old Stormalong

LIVING ABOARD old CONTENT has become almost pure delight, now that we no longer have to crack the ice to slide the main hatch back. I have to say "almost" because I've just discovered one more burden that owning this ponderous gaff rigger entails. (I'm not talking about dry rot or the bank note.) I'm talking about the burden of having acquired, and done so automatically, the public image of Old Stormalong simply by being "the guy who lives on that big old wooden boat." Now, a public image of, say, a shrewd businessman or superb unicyclist might not be too hard to bear but it appears that Old Stormalong is supposed to love foul weather. Ye Gods, foul weather scares the hell out of me! It always did. It scares me now worse than it ever did. I don't mind drowning, but one bad grounding with CONTENT and I'd ruin several sheets of copper sheathing. Sailing her is like sailing St. Paul's cathedral: you'd just hate to be the one to damage her.

I realized all this one day as I hunkered on deck, quaking with terror, pretending to serve a bit of rigging. It was one of those blustery spring days, blowing about 30 knots out of the southeast, grey ragged clouds tumbling along the sky. I was thankful that I was safe in port, though a bit worried lest my docklines should part. I was considering waiting out the weather in Denver when an acquaintance strolled by on the pier. "Boy, this is your kind of weather," he called out with the kind of enthusiasm that always gives me a headache. "Yeah, gotta work, though," I said, serving away like crazy.

There's no doubt that in strong breezes CONTENT is happiest but I'm not, at least not always. It's fine to go bowling down Long Island Sound with all kites flying; even *I* think I'm Old Stormalong then. But in order to get into the Sound you've got to get out of the damned harbor. Before you even do *that* you have to get away from the pier and CONTENT has no engine. I suppose it's not too hard to do any of that but I generally try to do it without involving the major public liability underwriters of the Eastern Seaboard. The maneuver involves docklines, anchors, assorted neighbors, and more than a dash of hysteria. A really stiff breeze from the wrong quarter can give one pause.

Coming home again, provided one gets out, can be even scarier in a breeze. We use bow and stern anchor to stop the old juggernaut, then lines rowed or thrown ashore to warp her in.

It's all a pretty maneuver except when it's "our kind of wind." Then, things that *Chapman's* didn't warn me about happen. You can *forget* how to tie a bowline when your anchor is dragging and people are telling you that your anchor is dragging and to get a bowline around "that piling over there." Why is it that an anchor can allow one to drag, usually toward the yachtsiest gold plater in the dock, yet be impossible to pick up when you're safe in the slip? What's old *Chapman's* got to say about that, eh?

So, CONTENT is turning me into an old lady. And I used to think of myself as something of a "driver." Indeed, I was, but a curious fact emerges as I dredge over past shoals. I was a "driver" mainly when sailing other people's boats. "My kind of weather" was breezing up and putting the lee rail under—*your* lee rail—*his*—lee rail.

In CONTENT, I'm not afraid of breaking rigging or gear; her forestay is ⅜-inch wire rope. I'm afraid of tipping over the kitty litter box, capsizing the laundry hamper, scrambling everything in the hanging locker. If my lee rail is buried, it's my home that's heeled 45 degrees. If I smash into headseas, it's all my worldly goods and chattels that are getting agitated (and some of the chattels can get *damned* agitated). A hard long beat on starboard tack may look picturesque to you but for me it can mean lopsided casserole for dinner. Nothing will so ruin the morale of the vessel's company as chattels agitated over a lopsided casserole.

If you see a lovely old gaff-rigged cutter under all sail on Long Island Sound this winter in a howling Norther it almost certainly won't be CONTENT or me. If it should be CONTENT, the reason won't be because Old Stormalong loves to careen around in northers; it'll be because he left on a mild day in August and has been afraid to attempt to come back through the breakwater entrance ever since.

CHAPTER 6

Distortion of the Commonplace

LIVING ABOARD has opened a door to another universe, a universe of strange variants of otherwise commonplace things. So far I've only discovered a few but I'm sure there are more—many more—waiting for me to slip on, trip over, and collide with. I don't mean just physical things, but those that jar the *psyche* as well as the left kneecap; those out of their natural order or slightly distorted, such as a dog that goes "meow" or archery equipment in a submarine.

For instance, all sailors have yelled or had yelled at them such yells as "starboard!" or "how much water over there?" But few have had occasion to yell, "sorry . . . pressure cooker!" The explanation for the yell (which never actually got yelled but for which there was a need) is that we often cook under sail; not heat-up-the-Van-Camp's-Pork-and-Beans cooking, but chop-vegetables-and-grease-the-baking-dish cooking. The case in point involved a pressure cooker. The relief valve of a pressure cooker won't go spittle-sputtle unless it is horizontal, and it never is on CONTENT unless we're broad off the wind or hauled out. Yet, it's supposed to go spittle-sputtle, and if we harden up it goes psss—or makes no noise at all, which is worse, I'm told. I recall bowling along gently with a 15-knot breeze on the starboard quarter and sighting another boat under my lee, same tack, close-hauled and closing fast. I yelled down to my gentle seawife that I'd have to harden up or even luff up to let a privileged boat by.

"Cut 'em in half!" she yelled back, "I've got a beef burgundy stew on!" (In fact, if memory serves, she also yelled "Hold yer course"—a locution she uses when emphatic *and* salty.) I held as long as I dared, then fell way off to go below the other boat, risking both rig and reputation for a few seconds because that necessitated sailing by the lee. Had we gybed, our boom would have cleaned off his deck house. By way of apology for yielding so late, I wanted to yell, "Sorry, but I couldn't luff up sooner because the relief valve on our pressure . . ." but you know the rest. Perhaps there is a flag signal for this situation but that chapter in *Chapman's* has long since mildewed. Anyway, there wasn't time. By the time I got my solitary "sorry!" the other boat was gone in a welter of profanity.

Related also to cooking and the commonplace-with-a-twist motif is the matter of bread. Doubtless you think you know all about bread. What the heck, there's pumpernickel, whole wheat, white, etc. Ah, but on CONTENT bread is sometimes baked under sail, giving rise not only to broad-reach bread but both port-tack and starboard-tack bread. Running-free bread is just barely feasible as long as it doesn't become following-sea bread. CONTENT's easy bilges let her roll heavily then, and the dough doesn't rise properly, producing something that would make excellent chart weights if only it could be cut.

Distortion of the commonplace is not relegated to sailing. It occurs right at the dock, plugged in to 110 volts AC and the rest of the world. Shoveling snow, for instance, entails a number of incongruities, not the least of which is the presence of a snow shovel on a sailing vessel. In addition, shoveling snow off a pier entails some peculiar problems. The discovery of one of which damn near destroyed my solar plexus.

I had decided that the easy way to shovel the snow off would be to get going fast with my pusher-type shovel and just zoom the snow off the edge of the pier. This I could do, thought I, by holding the end of the shovel handle securely against my belly and running like hell down the pier while pushing a great geyser of powdery snow ahead of me. It should have been easy. I've seen snowplows on Interstate 95 do it many times. I overlooked one thing. Nailheads. It wouldn't have been so bad if my maneuver had failed within the first few feet but it worked long enough for me to get up an impressive speed. When the blade of my shovel struck its first nailhead, I folded around the end of the handle like kelp around an anchor rode. My glasses were the only part of me to keep going, in accordance with Newton's First Law of Inertia.

The mishap led to a solution to the problem, which is yet another example of our theme. I soon adopted a precaution of hammering down and setting all protruding nails before a likely snowfall. That's a lot of work but it is a satisfactory solution. What strikes me as peculiar, though, is that I am the only person on the East Coast who prepares for a snowfall with a claw hammer and nail set.

CHAPTER 7

Dad the Deck Ape

THE SECOND SADDEST thing in the world is the sailor whose wife and child do not care for or understand sailing. The saddest thing in the world is the poor jerk whose wife and child not only care for and understand sailing, but who do so on a much more expert level than he does (to hear them tell it—and if you're around CONTENT very long you will), and who are not shy about letting him know it. That's the dark side of living aboard. You're not "Skipper" or "Cap"; you're just "Dad"—a term synonymous with "deck ape" under the best of circumstances and which varies in stature in inverse proportion to wind speed. At Force 6 in Block Island Sound it's on a par with terms used by Icelandic nomads to control the musk ox.

When I tell new acquaintances that I live aboard year round, they often comment on how "great" or "interesting" or even "adventurous" it must be. Now, CONTENT is a happy vessel—"a home and a feeder" as the Cape Horners used to say of a ship owned by benevolent backers or skippered by a kindly master—but there is certainly no "master" to be found. Certainly the burned out old geezer who carries the garbage up to the dumpster ashore every night is neither the master, nor "adventurous," nor even, for that matter, interesting. And the fellow who rolls out at 0500 to check the anchor rode when cruising the byways of Long Island Sound cannot be the master—a master would have ordered one of the crew to do that. No, there is no master to be found on CONTENT; there is what may be appropriately termed a loose confederation of three masters, each of whom enjoys absolute sovereignty at all times.

The trouble is that everyone aboard CONTENT knows pretty much what everyone else knows—there is no secret or arcane knowledge with which to awe the uninitiated. I tell you, the ancient Egyptian priests well knew what they were about when they closely guarded such secrets as the multiplication of fractions. The secret got out and now look where they are. Some skippers can squint up at a luff with an air of expertise that impresses their unsailorly wives or children. I can just hear such a wife telling her child in hushed tones,

"Stay here in the cockpit, Bernard, Daddy's doing something awfully important in the front of the boat." On CONTENT, if I just *look* as though I'm about to check the stays'l, my 10-year-old son is likely to say, "I eased her a bit, Dad, so you can stay put; fall off and lee-bow this ebb tide." When we cruise up the Sound on those short bright summer nights, I must tiptoe about the foredeck if I want to trim the sail, not because I don't want to wake the off watch, but because I'm not prepared to defend my actions in the verbal onslaught sure to follow waking them up. "Why are you hardening up?" "What are you doing shortening sail?" "Why isn't the yankee jib drawing better?" That's when I think back to the time when my new salty bride and I were doing some spring fitting out and she suddenly put down her scraper (hell, it might have been a broad axe—I forget), squinted skyward and said, "There's wind aloft; let's cast off and go sailing!" At the time, I was delighted. How many men have had the good fortune to marry women who say, "There's wind aloft." My God— "aloft." She really did say "aloft"—I swear it. What I didn't realize was that any woman who says "aloft" is not likely to be shy about putting her own two-cents' worth in when I want to make some change in sail trim in the middle of the night.

The same phenomenon has overtaken my son. There was a time when I used to look forward to being able to teach him all the sailing lore I know. Mental images designed by Norman Rockwell took over my fantasies. You know the sort: The old man and the boy in the lee of the longboat; learning to splice; sea stories in the fo'c's'le; the old salt explains chartwork.

Let me tell you what happened the first time I ever consciously set about to teach my son something about sailing. We had been charging up Fisher's Island Sound bound for Watch Hill, my son at the tiller. I saw that he was studying the small craft chart intently. "Aha! The old salt explains chartwork," I thought.

"Jamey, let me take the tiller and I'll tell you how to read a chart," I said.

"I know how to read a chart, Dad," he said, "I was just worried about getting set onto The Dumplings. Maybe we should come up to about 70 degrees."

"The Dumplings," said I, trying not to whimper, "what are you talking about? Who taught you to read a chart?"

"Dad," he said with great patience, "it's obvious."

"OK, wise guy, let me see that chart," I said.

I glanced at the chart.

"Come to . . . to . . . make it . . . oh . . . 70 degrees," I said, "and be quick about it."

I should have been proud, I guess, but at the time I was too pre-occupied with trying to figure out where in hell Watch Hill had gotten to—before Jamey gave me the course.

CHAPTER 8

Avert Eyes, Captain Offloading Garbage

THERE ARE CERTAIN traditional symbols of seasonal changes: The first robin of spring, the turning of leaves in the fall, etc. They leave me unmoved. Living aboard the old hooker has changed my outlook. The coming of winter is not marked for me by such traditional signs as frost on window panes and geese flying south. Oh, I still notice things; I just don't give a damn.

I'll tell you which winter signs matter to me. They've shut the bloody water off at the boatyard and my 12-volt bilge pumps no longer have the pizzazz they had in August. Also, my 14-pound tom-cat no longer lands on my solar plexus at four in the morning. That's because the porthole over my bunk is closed against the chill of the night and he can't jump down on me after a night's carouse.

In that respect I suppose I'm better off. From April to November I get landed on pretty regularly, and it's a great strain on a part of my anatomy one would not normally guess would be at hazard— my forehead. It's simple: the cat hits my belly and I involuntarily sit up, thumping my forehead on a deck beam. That's why I can't have a tell-tale compass. I figure my forehead would make contact at about N x ¼ E.

I suppose the foregoing shows that winter isn't all bad. Some of its signs and rituals even approach being downright pleasant. For one thing, when icicles droop from crackling docklines and skylights are frosted in the chill of a morning, it's nice to be free of the heavy and sometimes onerous duty to go sailing. I know . . . I know . . . We're not supposed to talk that way, are we? Wooden boat sailors especially are not supposed to talk that way. Sailing is *fun* and we must *love* it all the time. Well, lads—'fess up—you know that some-times *not* sailing is even more fun. And not sailing in the winter time is *really* fun.

Aboard CONTENT we have a number of winter rituals that go a long way toward making the long wait for the vernal equinox a bear-able wait. One of the more pleasant rituals is the making and drink-ing of mulled wine. There are only one or two things more pleasant than mulled wine in the winter time and this is neither the time nor the place to mention them. Imagine coming home in the dark, the cold, the wet, and crunching along the pier toward your boat. There's a cheery glow on the underside of the boom from the cabin lights. You slide back the hatch and a gentle breath of warm air enfolds you. But that ain't all. That breath is laden with the heady aroma of fresh cinnamon, lemon, burgundy, perhaps a touch of nutmeg. You're inside now, you close the hatch and the sound of the winter wind is instantly quelled, as if someone had turned off a radio. Your good seawife hands you a mug filled with the source of this lovely aroma. You sip it—almost too hot—but with eyes asquint and lips pursed you give it an expert slurp with plenty of air to just take the biting edge off the heat. Down goes that first little sip; its warmth is somehow more than a mere matter of BTUs. Ahh! Mulled wine!

Ice itself is not all bad, either. Yes, it pulls caulking out and scores planks along the waterline, but you can walk on it and when you drop things overboard, you can get them back—unless of course they are your car keys, in which case they will have fallen in the unfrozen two- or three-inch zone around the boat. Ice also flattens out wakes from the ash and gravel barges coming from the bowels (and I choose my words with precision) of Stamford.

Ice can also be a powerful force for moral rectitude afloat. How can this be? Easy. How often have you chucked something nasty overboard at night? Sure, I know, you generally are very conscientious about safeguarding the environment and we all decry the slaughter of the blue whale, but c'mon, guy—just one little beer can last July because the plastic bag with the day's garbage had already been tied shut? Just one little heave-ho with the kitty litter because you're in your pajamas already and it's too far to the dumpster? Just one sneaky flip up through the foredeck hatch with the melon rind? What the hell, how many whooping cranes is that gonna hurt?

You can't do it on ice, Charlie. The boo-boo will be there in the morning if you do. I know, because when we first got an engine for old CONTENT, I couldn't find the oil sump drain, and could think of no other way to get the oil out than to pump it out by opening an oil line and cranking the engine slowly with the batteries. Unfortunately, there was no practical way to collect the oil, so I let it drain into the bilge. I then filled the bilge with seawater and some super detergent for emulsifying anything. Then Nancy and I swung from the shrouds until CONTENT was rolling like a North Sea trawler, in effect making of her a giant cocktail shaker. Then, cowardly wretch that I am, I waited until about two in the morning and pumped the bilge. Then I went to sleep secure in the knowledge that I had hidden my crimes from mankind.

I had forgotten about the ice. The next morning I stuck my head out the hatch and saw that CONTENT was the center of a gigantic and hellish bubble bath. The oil and detergent mixture had been beaten into a froth by the bilge pump rotors. It was as if someone had pressed the button on a huge can of black Reddi-Whip. I tried shoveling it toward a neighbor's boat but it was like trying to shovel feathers. Finally I got rid of it by running the engine, and the hot water in the exhaust melted enough of the ice to allow the glop to dissipate in the water. But for the rest of the winter CONTENT was the only boat in the yard surrounded by brown ice.

That persistent evidence of my sins so traumatized me that I never throw anything overboard without first checking to make sure the surrounding water isn't the hard kind.

CHAPTER 9

If Winter Comes, Can Spring Be Far Behind?

THE TIME OF the malfunctioning bubbler system, burst water tank, and ice-stopped galley sink drain is upon us, and once again my thoughts turn to that traditional old bedrock of the liveaboard wooden boat sailor—plastic. Oh, it's all very well for you to cry, "For shame!" at this seeming fall from grace, as you read this in your warm house, enjoying the comforts of standing headroom. But I'm sitting here in the main cabin, ice-bound on this frozen coast, waiting for my distal appendages to slough off.

I have observed that the most virulently purist of the purists are those who do not live aboard. I mean no insult here; living aboard in the winter, in fact, can only be explained in terms of psychopathology. I mean simply that people who, through one genetic defect or another, *do* live aboard soon learn to take their pathetic little comforts where they can, even if that does mean putting sandwich baggies over the hawsepipes. In this way the traditionalist owes what little winter comfort he can salvage to modern chemistry.

Even from afar, poor old CONTENT, with her blue DuPont tarpaulin covering her completely, looks like some monument to the age of plastics; she certainly bears no resemblance to a sailing vessel. But every night, when I go beddy bye 'neath my plastic electric blanket, I'm thankful for the added warmth and ice-free decks afforded by that other plastic affront to nautical purity. To complete the picture of some outlandish seagoing leaf bag, we have covered our skylights (Good God! Our fine old teak skylights!) with white plastic trashcan liners. We could have used green but that would have clashed with the blue of the tarpaulin. The entire visual ensemble is tastefully set off by our snow shovel propped forward of the mast. The shovel is raked aft. I have always believed that a plumb snow shovel is the mark of a lubber.

The plastic cover over the skylights provides a dead air space, which conserves heat. It also shuts out such bothersome sights as geese flying across the azure sky, the crisp bright moon on a winter's night, and the sun sparkling on icicles hanging from the rigging. It gives the impression, on going below, of becoming entombed, which is entirely accurate. Before the plastic, though, I would wake up each morning to breakfast under skylights with several millimeters of frost on the inside. As the morning coffee and my quivering body warmed the cabin, the frost would melt. I tolerated this for a long time before I realized that my coffee tasted lousy not because I make lousy coffee (in fact I make *atrocious* coffee) but because there was bedding compound in it. There was bedding compound in it because the effluent from the skylights was leaching it from the glass bedding and carrying it drip by drip into my cup. True, I could have solved the immediate problem by moving my cup, but I figured that if we were losing enough heat through the skylights to allow the formation of hoar frost, the laws of thermodynamics were trying to tell me something.

The necessary intrusion of plastic extends even further into our interior decor, if decor is what you can call what we've got. I can sympathize with an acquaintance who visited us recently and was put off by the outdoor carpeting on our cabin sole. After all, he came to the boat expecting to see a boat. What he saw as he approached was a blue plastic excrescence on the water, with snow shovel (raked aft) and white plastic lumps where he had been accustomed to seeing skylights. He climbed aboard, snaked under the plastic, and slid back the hatch.

What did he see? Our salty old wideplank polished-oak cabin sole? He did not. He saw the inside of a Rent-All Camper. A snow shovel may be excused, I suppose; one does have to shovel the pier. But a 67-year-old English pilot cutter with wall-to-wall carpeting? Well, even the carpeting would be allowed by any purist who knew what life aboard was like without it. Formerly, the bare sole would allow cabin heat to draw Arctic air up from the bilge, so that one was constantly walking around as if ankle deep in ice water. Make that knee deep. The rugs cut that circulation off enough to allow us to sit like regular people instead of spending from January to April with our legs hunkered up under our chins like a family of baboons.

I close with a simple thought. When we awaken aboard CON-TENT after, say, eight hours without heat (for safety we shut off all heat but the electric blanket at night), the cabin temperature may be at a level that would permit me to step into any randomly selected commercial meat freezer to warm up. Chew on that before shaking your head at our shameless use of plastic to sustain life until the vernal equinox.

CHAPTER 10

The Finest Wing-Tip Seaboots for Office and Shipboard

L OTS OF BOOKS address the problems of the liveaboarder, but not one treats the most fundamental problem of the chap who lives aboard and also holds a traditional full-time job ashore. I refer to the problems of alienation, the crazy incongruity between the two lives such a man must lead. Even as I write, seated at my desk in my office, surrounded by inter-office memos, telephone message forms—Ed Freemish can't make it on Thursday—and file cabinets, I know that in an hour I'll be worrying about chafed springlines. Hell, I'm worrying about them *now*, when I should be attending to that Freemish problem.

The trouble is that I can't do two things at once. It's that there's such an incredibly different *feeling*, different *atmosphere*, attached to springlines on the one hand, and Ed Freemish on the other. I have but to walk out on the pier to feel free, a bit rakish. By the time I swing aboard (I grab a shroud and sort of half step, half swing aboard, but I don't really have to), I'm feeling positively salty. But at the office, I feel . . . I feel just the way you feel at the office. But it's tougher for me, you see, because just a few hours or even a few minutes ago, I felt free, rakish, and salty. It's a shock to the system just to come to work in the morning.

The two worlds are completely different. I am constantly surprised at how little the shore life has to do with life afloat. I have had shore friends aboard who did not know which end of the boat was the bow, and CONTENT is no double-ender. A man in a grocery store who knew I lived aboard once asked me how I was going to get my grocery bags aboard. He was amazed to learn that I could just walk aboard. (I could *swing* aboard without the bags.) When I got married I had to explain to my new father-in-law that I went to work every morning with a briefcase. I felt it was very important to emphasize that briefcase . . . my badge of normalcy, you understand.

The incongruity between the two worlds is never more intense than when one is doing some shore-going thing immediately after completing a sail, especially a longish sail, a weekend cruise, let's say, in which thick weather has been encountered. I can recall thrashing home one Sunday evening against one of those sharp autumn nor'westers in Long Island Sound and then, almost within the hour of making CONTENT fast to the pier, sitting in my office getting some notes ready for a Monday morning conference. It's difficult to convey the profound difference in the two atmospheres, but suppose you were walking in the Maine woods and you encountered a door, passed through it, and found yourself in the waiting room of a dentist in Sandusky, Ohio?

The atmospheric distance between the two worlds is made even more telling by their physical proximity. CONTENT is docked only 100 yards or so from a tennis club, but going from one to the other is like that Sandusky-Maine woods passage, and that's why I hardly ever enter the tennis club.

Ashore, I am always aware of this alienation. I can have problems at 8 a.m. that I can't even tell anyone about at 9 a.m. because only a sailor would understand. For instance, my office friends occasionally come in late because the car didn't start or the basement flooded or they had to stay home to let the meter reader in. They can explain this to the boss in a few words. But I was late last week because a loose bight of my stays'l halyard, which I had unreeved for the winter, got foul of the piling at the end of the pier. (Try that on the boss.) I was awakened in the wee hours of the morning by a powerful thump followed by a shaking of the boat as if a giant hand were gripping the mast. I tumbled up on deck in my winter long johns to discover that the halyard had been flipped over the head of the piling by the blustery wind. It had probably happened during high tide, but now, as the tide had fallen a few feet, the bight of ½-inch Dacron, its standing part affixed to the masthead, had drawn up taut as a crowbar and as the line sporadically slipped over the rough surface of the piling, it jerked and shook the forestay, which in turn shook the whole boat. I suppose I'm lucky it awakened me when it did. Otherwise, the falling tide and increasing tension might eventually have taken out the topmast. And that would have been hard enough to explain to sailors, let alone landsmen. ("Sorry, I'm late, boss, but I was dismasted this morning right at the dock.")

I have tried to ease the incongruity between my two worlds by superimposing aspects of one upon the other. For instance, I am sitting here, as I said, at my desk, and anyone would take me for an OK fellow—normal. But under my desk is a 30-foot roll of sheathing copper, a five-gallon jug of Stockholm tar, and my seaboots. They're not helping.

CHAPTER 11

Surely, You Remember Houses

L IVING ABOARD this old girl CONTENT is OK, I guess, if you've got a natural bent for anguish and heartache, but the worst problem our lifestyle entails is the frequent feeling that we are impostors. My good seawife and I don't feel that way when we're aboard; we feel that way when we re-enter the world of normal, right-thinking, sensible people. That is to say, the world of people who live in houses. Surely, you remember houses.

I'm not talking about just going ashore. Land sakes, we go ashore to the 7-Eleven whenever the Fritos or other basic cruising staples run low; and we feel no sense of impostorship when we do, because the store—and many places ashore for miles around—is really part of the sailing world. I'm talking about going ashore to a home or a place of business or amusement that has nothing to do with boats, a place where I may put on a suit and Nancy may wear a dress, high-heeled shoes, and even earrings.

Then, we are impostors. We are dressed up like nice people, but we live aboard an old wooden boat. I realized this the first time I saw Nancy, all gussied up, stepping ashore from the bowsprit as we prepared to go to an antique auction at Sotheby's in New York City. There she was, looking like a southern belle, except that she was standing on a whisker stay and hanging on to the topmast stay and saying, "Step on that forward spring, will you, so I can get ashore." I did so, and took her arm as she stepped ashore; and then, to my everlasting regret, I replied, "My dear, you look just like a *real* lady."

Everything seems to have gone downhill since then, but all I meant was . . . was . . . oh, the hell with it.

Let me put it this way. All during that afternoon, that urbane and sophisticated afternoon (I mean, we had sangria in the park!), I kept thinking to myself, "All these people . . . they don't know . . . they think we're OK . . . they think we are one of them. Two hours ago my southern belle was stepping off a bowsprit, and I was blighting the rest of my life with an infelicitous choice of words."

Another time, we were at a cocktail party, attendance at which was important for the sake of my continued capacity to earn money with my typewriter. Naturally, we were disguised as regular people. People would talk to us and, of course, ask about what we did, where we lived. I would coolly reply that I wrote and lived in Fort Lauderdale. But sometimes people would press on until I found myself mumbling, "Well, actually, we live on a boat."

One fellow, more persistent than the rest, probed on relentlessly, and I heard myself saying, "No, not a houseboat; it's even worse than that. We live on an old wooden sailboat." I felt as if we had blown our cover. I would not have been surprised had conversation in the room stopped, faces had turned toward us in horror and disdain, and we had been lynched on the spot. I needn't have worried, though, for so outlandish had my statement been, apparently, that it never registered with my interrogator. It was as if I had said, "No, not a houseboat; we live in a large wooden shoe in the heart of the Black Forest." My interrogator turned to his wife and said, "Hey, hon, I want you to meet some interesting people. They live on a houseboat."

So, for the rest of the evening, we were the people who lived on a houseboat in Fort Lauderdale. In fact, as the evening passed, the houseboat moved to Bahia Mar in Fort Lauderdale; it was that kind of party. Talk about feeling like an impostor! I was forced to fill in all sorts of realistic details about life at Bahia Mar. I know as much about life at Bahia Mar as I do about life at the estate of the Archduke of Serbia. I do remember that the people at Bahia Mar once had the good sense not to let me tie up there overnight. We would have ruined the neighborhood.

Nancy is more open and forthright than I am about our dubious and suspect status as boat dwellers and so escapes much of the sense of being an impostor. We'll enter the home of a new acquaintance, all set for a civilized shore-type evening with people who think we're OK, and she'll exclaim, "Oh, what a great bathroom you have; do you mind if I take a shower?" Of course, no one ever minds, and people who live ashore always have showers that work, but they look at you funny when you have to ask to have a shower. Now, I too would love to take a shower without having to schlepp up to the boatyard shower behind the 7-Eleven with my soap and towel and stand around watching the Travel-Lift while waiting for someone to come out of the shower room, but I'm just not honest enough to come right out with a request that I know will lead straight to the blowing of my cover.

So, Nancy gets to take a shower while I sit there holding my scotch and soda and answering those "Oh-isn't-that-fascinating"-type questions about living on a wooden boat. (Incidentally, I would rather have had a rum, neat, no ice, but people ashore either don't drink rum or have never tasted the real thing in the Caribbean, so I never ask for rum when we go out to visit, unless I know the people really well.)

Sometimes, I admit, I blow my own cover, but never on purpose. I don't go around bumming showers. But sometimes passion of the moment overcomes my normal caution.

Once, we were sitting around in someone's living room, waiting for Nancy to come out of the shower. We were sipping the first of the evening's drinks and idly watching the weather report on television. The questions about my wife's eccentricities hadn't started yet. There had been a line of severe thundersqualls coming up the coast. The forecaster smilingly reassured his listeners that the storm front had changed course and was now ". . . safely out to sea." I began to rant and rave about the self-centeredness of the phrase, to describe the agonies of some poor bastard out there, rail under, one half scared and the other half terrified, trying to claw down his staysail luff.

I might as well have been talking to people from Jupiter. I certainly didn't make a good impression, although I didn't think I behaved so badly as to justify our never being invited back. Oh, well. As far as our hosts were concerned, I may have been an impossible grouch; but, boy, did I have a clean wife!

CHAPTER 12

A Sound Mind

IF LIVING ABOARD this old gaffer CONTENT has done nothing else for me (and it probably hasn't), it has made me exquisitely sensitive to sounds. Sounds, at least those heard aboard this boat, are almost always pregnant with meaning, with high significance for my future, usually my immediate future. A clanging bell, for instance, probably means that the sonofabitch really is going to raise the bridge in time. A single "galoop" sound, on the other hand, probably means that I now need yet another extension for my socket wrench, and that I am about to increase my knowledge of the streets of the southeastern United States by looking for a hardware store open on Sunday.

CONTENT's deep hull functions like a sonar receiver, enabling one to hear boat noises from far off. An outboard motor, for instance, makes a hissing sound something like air escaping from a tire, when the source is almost a mile away. More than once I have awakened in the middle of the night—in my sleepy state alarmed that air was escaping from one of my tires—only to hear the occupants of a motorboat shrieking to each other.

Then, when I stick my head out the hatch, I hear nothing for a few seconds. Finally, the far-off sound of an outboard motor can be heard, and the boat's crew still screaming at each other. I used to think that the phenomenon of people in outboards screaming at each other was due to their bad tempers—but now I realize it is due to hearing impairment. I am much more tolerant now that I understand this.

My developed sensitivity to sound is quite impressive—even, at times, uncanny. Outboard motors are not the only things that hiss, and I can usually differentiate among the various sources, sometimes without ever having heard that particular source before. For instance, one quiet night in a peaceful cove, I was awakened by a soft hiss. Something told me, and told me instantly, that this was the hiss of marsh grasses brushing softly along my hull. Now, that's OK if you're in a catamaran or even a catboat, but in a plank-on-edge English cutter drawing eight feet, marsh grass brushing along the hull ain't good. In fact, as soon as I heard it I heard an internal voice say, "Oh God—another damn anecdote in the making!"

I've forgotten the events that followed (but just ask my son, who keeps a file of all Dad's mistakes), but the point I wanted to make is that although I had never run ashore through marsh grass before, there was something unmistakably marsh grassish about that hissing noise. It could never have been mistaken for the hiss of a distant outboard—certainly never for the "galoop" of a socket wrench extension falling into the bilge.

I believe there is something of mysterious and cosmic significance in all this. How did I *know* that the sound was marsh grass, if I'd never before heard it? Are humans born with innate memories— if that's the word—of things that haven't happened to them yet? If hatchling turtles can crawl unerringly toward a sea they have never seen, if chicks shy away from a hawk's shadow even though they've never seen a hawk, maybe we are all born with the ability to identify the sound of marsh grass sliding past our hulls. I don't know where this leaves humans who are not sailors.

Perhaps it works both ways. Maybe we are all born with the un-tapped ability to identify the sound of a malfunctioning Jacuzzi or a stock broker in rutting season. Quien sabe?

Some people have failed to tap this innate ability—assuming it exists. You'd think that everyone would be able to identify the creak-ing sound that sailing vessels in pirate movies make, but, alas, this is not so. Incidentally, CONTENT has never made those sounds and I'd be very worried if she did, especially under sail, but I can imitate the sound to perfection. I gave my "olden time ship" sound imitation one lunch hour for some new acquaintances, landsmen who thought living aboard "interesting." After my first two or three deep, drawn-out creaking croaks, they were staring at me in horror. Too late did I realize that to anyone not nautically attuned, or too damn young to remember Errol Flynn in *Captain Blood*, the sound I was making had gastrointestinal rather than nautical associations. I tried to ex-plain about rigging and strains on the hull, but it only seemed to make things worse. I never got invited to lunch again.

It serves me right, I guess, for trying to "do" a sound that CON-TENT never makes. Next time, I'll stick to reality. I'm trying to come up with the sound of my checking account being overdrawn.

CHAPTER 13

Cutting the Umbilical

ANY NUMBER OF magazine articles instruct the reader about living aboard with animals. In CONTENT, we consider ourselves animal lovers and have always had pets. Currently, most of our animals are roaches, but that can usually be said of any boat in South Florida. Next in number come the humans, then the cats. Actually, there may be room for dispute about ranking the two cats after the three humans, for the classification of our teenage son (Homo sapiens) may be a taxonomic error. If the species name is supposed to be descriptive, then how about *H. smartassiensis*? The traditional classification as "human" may be an abuse of language. Why are there no magazine articles about living aboard with this bizarre form of marine life, the teenage boat person?

The answer may well be that no one has anything constructive to say about the subject. Perhaps we should simply slip the docklines when he's at school and sail to Bora Bora. Or, we could tie a little catboat astern, have him live in that, and not let him out until he's 37 and vice president of a midwestern insurance agency. Spending his life in a small boat until age 37 would not hinder his development, because he already knows everything. In addition, it would allow *us* to develop.

It is stultifying to the spirit of parents just beginning to enjoy the first fruits of senility to be told several times a day, "That's pretty dumb, Mom," or "Wrong again, Dad." I know that that sort of thing is also a problem for people who live ashore, but it is magnified aboard a boat.

There are so many things to do wrong aboard a boat. To enter a house you just open the door and go in. To enter CONTENT's main cabin you must step on a bowline, grab the forestay, step nimbly aboard, make your way down the deck without tripping over the hose that a certain person who shall go nameless didn't coil and hang up in the rigging, climb down the ladder and then . . . only then, are you "home." If you can do that in the presence of a teenager, at least *our* teenager, without invoking an epic monologue about all the ways you are doing it wrong, then the teenager is obviously a victim of a rare disease that paralyzes the vocal cords.

There is a corollary to the old saw that no man is a hero to his valet: no man is a skipper to his teenage son. If a real skipper gives the order to let go the anchor, you listen for the splash. If CONTENT's so-called skipper (the old dimwit) gives the order to let go the anchor, you listen for the rebuttal. We're anchoring in the wrong place, going too fast or not fast enough, or the moon is in the wrong phase. Success in anchoring, lying comfortably all night without dragging or excessive motion, would be attributed to dumb luck.

Failure, which would include a barking dog ashore or a half-point rise in the prime rate, would be attributed to another one of Dad's blunders.

I have no doubt that as the little crumb matures, he will gradually become aware that his father is a model of nautical wisdom, insight, and skill, but sometimes it seems as though it's going to be a long row to hoe. For instance, I was pleased recently to see in him the first stirrings of an interest in literature. He admitted liking some of the works of Hemingway and Fitzgerald, and some of the Greek myths. Aha, thought I. This is the beginning of his maturity. Soon he will have a functioning forebrain. We'll be pals.

Not long after, I went back to his cabin (the little fink has a cabin all to himself; Mom and Dad have to share a cabin) to see why I had heard no sarcasm from him in the last half-hour. He was asleep, a smile on his face and an open textbook beside him . . . Greek myths. Curious, I became intrigued by what he had been reading that had caused him to sashay off into the arms of Morpheus with such pleasure. You guessed it—summaries of the principal legends of ancient kings and gods, a good many of whom wiled away the hours by killing, castrating, and otherwise inconveniencing their fathers.

I repeat, sometimes it seems as if it's going to be a long row to hoe.

CHAPTER 14

The Rules of the Game

UNTIL A RELATIVELY short time ago English convicts were sent to superannuated colliers and other old wooden craft anchored in the Thames estuary. The practice was sometimes called "being sent to the hulks." Ten years ago, my good seawife and I voluntarily moved from an 11-room farmhouse into an old wooden hulk, and we had never been convicted of anything more serious than virulent romanticism. I knew there would be adjustment problems, especially in the matter of privacy as our son grew older. I didn't realize the unlikely source from which light was to be shed on this problem.

I have learned much about the maintenance of privacy from observing our two cats. Now cats, as cat lovers know in their heart of hearts but are too goody-goody to admit, are dumb . . . dumb as hell. The only thing dumber than a cat is a smart horse. So, cats don't solve problems by using smarts; they solve problems by exercising stupidity . . . but stupidity of a special kind.

Allow me to explain. Our cats hate each other, probably because they are opposites in almost all respects. One is thin, brave, the essence of cattishness. The other is a fat, cowardly wimp, a cat in outward form only. Yet these two manage to share the same feeding bowl, kitty litter box, and other facilities, and only rarely do they get in each other's way.

How do they accomplish this? By simply not noticing each other . . . by sheer unadulterated obtuseness. One simply does not see the other on its way to the feeding dish, even though the hungry one passes only a few feet away. Occasionally the system breaks down, as when they practically walk into each other. Then there is a mighty yowling and screeching, but they usually succeed in maintaining their incredible feline insensitivity to each other's existence.

Now, what cats can do through brutishness, humans can do through the exercise of intelligent willpower. We can maintain our privacy by choosing not to see each other when it is impolitic to do so. Of course, we get some concrete privacy by way of the boat's interior layout. After all, the head is not really located out in the

39

middle of the main cabin. It only seems that way, especially when there are guests for dinner. Even though there is a door on the head (well of course there's a door . . . we're not savages!), the "facility"—to put it delicately—is close enough to the main cabin to require something else in order to bolster the feeling of privacy. That's where the human intelligent will comes in. The tacit rule on CONTENT is that anyone who is in the head does not exist. It is an especially serious gaffe to include such a person in the main-cabin discussion by asking him direct questions, such as requesting him to give the main antecedents and subsequent socioeconomic effects of the Smoot-Hawley Tariff.

That general rule applies to other situations as well. If people are changing their clothes, they temporarily drop out of the universe. They become unobservable, like a black hole . . . or one cat on its way to the food bowl, while another is snoozing right above it on the settee.

That mental exercise transcends all interior layouts devised by the cleverest naval architects. The ability to switch people on and off is where real privacy resides. Without it, no small boat affords real privacy. With it, people can have privacy in a telephone booth. (Well, maybe not a telephone booth . . . one needs some help. There is, after all, that door on the head.)

The ability to selectively switch parts of the real world on and off may be useful in other problem-solving situations. Years ago, when my son was a child, we would tether him to the mast by a long rope whenever we sailed. The rope allowed him complete access to the boat, above and below, but was an effective safety device. We insisted that whenever he had friends aboard for an afternoon sail that they, too, wear a long tether.

One day, my son and two friends became bored and decided that a game of hide-and-seek would be pleasant. As we were still sailing, we refused permission to remove the tethers. The three children solved the problem with the brilliance that seems to be the special province of genius and foolishness. They played hide-and-seek for hours (on a 40-foot boat, for goodness' sake!), with the following rule added to the usual rules of the game: The tethers don't exist; no fair noticing the tethers.

There has always seemed to me something mystically wonderful about that feat, like that of the Zen master supposedly so wise that he could imagine a stick with only one end, or not think about a white bear. I have not mentioned this sense of wonder to my son, because at 16 he would simply explain that the feat is easy for him and wonderful to me because of his greater mental power. I can hear him telling me how even our cats do something similar and that, of course, our cats think *I'm* pretty dumb.

CHAPTER 15

A Most Excellent Leak

SEVERAL DAYS AGO I realized that I live on a boat. I know I should have realized this fact a long time ago; as a matter of fact, I was aware of it until a few years back, when somehow it slipped my mind. I knew I lived on a boat back in the days when we did things like—just imagine—sailing. For the past two years, though, we've been in the dock while I have been engaged in the manufacture of sawdust and the subsidy of the marine hardwoods industry of South Florida.

During this extensive period we have gradually become more like trailer (oops—I must learn to say "mobile home") park tenants than sailors. We make telephone calls from our *two* phones, dash out for groceries, go to work in morning traffic, receive mail—all the things that a million years of evolution have brought us to and none of which has the slightest smell of the sea about it. I mean, a lot has been written about, say, Herman Melville and Joseph Conrad, but no one has ever or will ever suggest that they ever took out the garbage. We do plenty of domestic stuff, but we hardly ever do anything salty. Oh, once in a while I shake the forestay and squint aloft, but the action has no practical purpose; it's like a cat going through the motions of covering its dung even though it has just defecated on a concrete floor.

Therefore, I was delighted recently when I was reminded that CONTENT really isn't a Winnebago. That reminder came at about 4 a.m. (see, I forgot how to say "0400"), when she sprang a most excellent leak.

Now, there are leaks, and there are leaks. There are leaks that announce their presence with a slight increase in the triggering of the automatic bilge pump. More impressive are leaks that one can see as a rivulet. Further upscale are leaks that produce a visible up-welling in the bilge. But my leak—ah, my leak was a leak that one could hear. An audible leak—now, there's a leak that a man can really become involved with.

Of course, the leak woke me up at 0400. (Every significant event in a sailor's life happens at 0400.) As I crawled aft still half asleep, fearful, nervously clutching a malfunctioning flashlight (someday, someone will invent a flashlight that works, and he shall be exalted above all the sons of Abraham), I thought, even through my dread, "'Gad, sir, this is what yachting is all about!" I hadn't felt so nautically alive since I last ran aground in Long Island Sound, having mistaken Venus for Stratford Shoal light. (Hell, it probably wasn't even Venus.)

Of course, I felt even better when I spotted the leak and saw that it was in a place I could reach, just above the stuffing box. As I gently pushed cotton into the seam (some caulking had let go—at least, I hoped that was all it was), it occurred to me that if I wasn't having much fun, at least I was engaged in the most nautical activity that I'd performed in more than two years.

Pushing caulking into a seam from the inside may offend the purist, but I am happy to report that it prevents outside water from becoming inside water, which is also what boating is all about. In my particular case, there even turned out to be a nautical precedent. As I pushed on the caulking cotton, I could feel that the area around the leak was not wood. Then, under the fitful flashlight beam, I could just discern little mounds of venerable, old rubbery glop. Finally, sure enough—there were ancient bits of ancient caulking cotton that somehow I was not surprised to encounter. Once again, I had been repeating history. Some unknown former skipper had made an unconventional repair, but had added the refinement of glop over caulking. Disgraceful, of course, but it *had* held for 11 to 70 years. Once again, I had uncovered one of CONTENT's secrets.

I had also intensified my personal sense of having lived aboard a boat all these years. Being forced to make a lubberly emergency repair to an older makeshift repair had the effect of uniting me in fellow lubberliness to my unknown predecessor. In fact, so strong is the kinship that I'm getting second thoughts about my initial resolve to make a proper repair when CONTENT is hauled. Maybe I should just pour on more glop from the inside—in order to carry on the tradition.

CHAPTER 16

A Midwinter Morale Booster

NOW IS THE season when I can make use of one of the most potent morale boosters I know: the gleeful contemplation of the misfortunes of others. And being a sailor during the winter anywhere north of the 35th parallel of latitude is a grave misfortune. If you happen to be a liveaboard sailor, multiply the previous observation by a scale factor of at least 2.743.

As I sit here perspiring slightly beneath rustling palm trees, it does my black heart good to think of some poor bastard up in New England arguing with the yard manager because the bubble maker didn't go on again last night and ice has already formed around his schooner. I can hear it now: "Whaddiyah *mean* the man to fix the thermostat will be in on Thursday? I'm losing my caulking compound *now*!"

Some of my Northern winter memories are pleasant, of course, and I do sometimes miss the change of the seasons. However, we have seasonal changes down here below the Smith and Wesson Line. Our seasonal changes are just a bit more subtle. For instance, the onset of winter in South Florida is marked by a dramatic increase in rates at the Bahia Mar and the Marriott marinas. In New England, you have the fall colors—different folks, different strokes.

Preparing for winter aboard up North was always fun. There were those weekend trips to the hardware store for plastic "tarps," snow shovels, extra fuses, etc. The plastic was for erecting a cover over the boat. The properly prepared boat looked like a blue Mongolian yurt. (Some people had orange plastic. Their boats looked like orange Mongolian yurts.) The snow shovel was to replace last year's snow shovel. Last year's snow shovel had been lent to the young couple aboard the cutter GRANOLA, last reported with a large red sticker on her mast at a sheriff's auction in New London. The extra fuses were for replacing the already exhausted supply of extra fuses. Winter causes fuse boxes to develop an insatiable craving for fuses. I'm no electrician, but I'm pretty sure it has something to do with their metabolism.

I can recall those little gasps of surprise as winter deepened, when, upon opening the hatch in the morning, one discovered yet another piling lying on its side atop the ice, having been plucked out of the bottom mud by the ice rising on the flood tide. One could see pilings canted at every crazy angle all over the harbor. It was fun wondering when one's own piling would be next.

Of course, we always tried to keep our own dock's piling clear of ice, a task much facilitated by the fact that virtually all of our so-called bubble berth came up right around the piling that held our finger pier in place. That arrangement also eliminated that hazardous ice-free zone around the boat's hull, into which an unwary ice skater might have fallen. In addition, being locked solidly into a harbor-sized sheet of ice somewhat reduced the shock transmitted to us whenever the garbage tug went by. We had learned that keeping the ice clear with a shovel allowed the ice sheet to "get a run" at us, so to speak, when the tug went by pushing a quarter-acre of hardened Long Island Sound at us. We soon saw the wisdom of allowing the ice to form solidly right up to the hull. That way, one would sort of surge toward the suction of the tug's prop, then surge away as the tug passed. After a while, we got so used to it that we didn't fall down much.

It was lonely living aboard during winter. Most people had gone to their warm houses and only came down to the marina to check on their boats. That is, checking on their boats was the excuse they gave. Their real reason was to partake of the excellent hot spiced wine often to be found aboard CONTENT. On the other hand, we would often visit them in their warm houses, ostensibly to—well—just to visit, but getting a nice, hot shower somehow often became part of the visit. I think this sort of thing is called symbiosis.

Of course, we had washing facilities on CONTENT. We had soap. We had water. We had a 2x4 feet galvanized tub. Washing was a real chore. The steam would condense on the skylights and then freeze during the night. The next morning, when I fired up the stove, the ice would melt and drip into my coffee. I got quite good at making my coffee just strong enough to allow for the subsequent dilution factor.

If one wanted some privacy when bathing, one could use the shower stall ashore. If you want to know what willpower is, I can tell you: It's trudging 500 yards up an icy pier on a bitter February evening to take a shower in an unheated plywood shack. I'm here to tell you that there are lots worse things in life than being a little dirty for a few weeks.

I don't want to be smug about the hardships of winter in Northern climes, though. After all, we have our own problems down
South. If you leave a tool in the sun for more than a minute, it'll be
too hot to pick up. And the roaches here are big enough to vote. I
can get heat stroke working on CONTENT in the middle of winter, but
I'd probably feel the warning signs early enough to stop and get
some water. Up North, I'd be too damn numb to feel anything.

CHAPTER 17

The Pleasure of Pets on Board

SOME OF US who own wooden boats have been remiss in not sharing with the rest of the class the joys of pet ownership while living aboard. As the past proud proprietor of two, count 'em, Weimaraners, I can tell you that the pleasures of pets on board are second only to those of root-canal work or bus travel with children.

As CONTENT made her stately way up and down Long Island Sound, we grew as accustomed to cries of "beautiful dogs" as we were to "beautiful boat." To the former, we often replied "Wanna buy 'em?" but received no offers. Perhaps we should have offered the familiar "buy one . . . get one free" enticement. What these spectators couldn't see, of course, was the grubby reality beneath the outward show. Beautiful dogs sitting side by side on the foredeck with their intelligent faces in the wind make a pretty picture, but cleaning dog hairs out of the bilge pump does not and wondering who in hell ate the last of the stew does not.

And speaking of things that do not make a pretty picture, try rowing two frantic 80-pound dogs ashore on what you hope is a deserted beach at 0300 so that they can do what a Weimaraner's gotta do. I know that sounds awful, I mean the environment and all and save-the-snail-darter and stuff, but whatcha gonna do when the dock you tried to dinghy up to five hours ago turned out to belong to the "Old Quiet Money Yacht Club," which does not allow dogs? (Nor, I suspect, do they allow humans who couldn't trace their families back to the Thames prison hulks.) At any rate, their dockmaster had asked if I were a registered member, in a tone that had caused the moisture in that summer air to freeze. I remember the tinkle of ice crystals falling on the pier as vividly as if it were only yesterday.

I recall that the dogs, later that night, seemed to sense my desire to accomplish their defecatory mission with utmost stealth. They sat quietly in the stern of the dinghy as I rowed ashore. They stepped ashore daintily, like ballerinas, instead of splashing wildly as they normally did. After relieving themselves, they hopped as quietly back aboard and waited for me to dispose of the evidence. My method was to carefully scoop their calling cards onto the oar end and catapult them seaward. I don't believe I ever hit another boat, although I do recall one night during the dark of the moon when I did not hear the expected splash of my missile but instead an outraged "Goddammit!" from somewhere out there in the murk of Cuttyhunk anchorage. I feel guilty about it, and if this text ever falls in front of the wrong eyes I suppose my butt will be in a sling, but the poor bastard should have had an anchor light. (That's another fine point you won't find in *Chapman's*.)

If the foregoing doesn't motivate you to rush out and procure a dog or two for your boat, perhaps I can interest you in a cat. We have owned a series of cats on CONTENT, including some whose sentences ran concurrently with our dogs. Some people think that cats are more fitting on wooden boats and that they are less trouble.

As to the first, I believe that that canard gained currency merely because yacht designers are better at drawing cats than they are dogs. As to the second, it's a toss-up. You don't have to row cats ashore at 0300, but dogs don't decide to attack your body parts at that hour, apparently mistaking one of them for a small animal scurrying about under the sheet. You can't train cats not to do this because you can't train cats. You can't train cats because they are dumb. The only thing dumber than a cat is bottom paint.

Cats also have a habit of bringing their owners presents. This is cute and touching, especially if you are fond of partially dismembered small vertebrates. People who live in houses are well acquainted with this feline habit, but people who live on small boats have a special relationship to it. Frequently one's boat cat leaves such a present out of sight. No matter, in a few days one's olfactory sense kicks in where vision failed. The search that ensues can rival the intensity of a search for a leak on a dark night in thick weather.

I have seen some boats with parrots aboard. That might seem a better choice than either dogs or cats, but I doubt it. Parrots may seem more traditional, of course, especially if you intend to prey on East Indiamen out of Port Royale, but parrots, although certainly smarter than cats, are also crazy. I once belonged to a sailing club that had a pet parrot that would go berserk if it heard a woman's voice raised any louder than a whisper. It would begin to shriek "Oh my" and attack anything that moved.

Can you imagine what it would be like if you were trapped on a boat with such a bird? And what about cleanliness? Can you boatbreak a bird? I don't think so. You'd probably have to anchor off a beach at night. On the other hand, the parrot could fly ashore, and the missiles would be smaller than those of a Weimaraner. . . .

PART TWO

Sailing
CONTENT

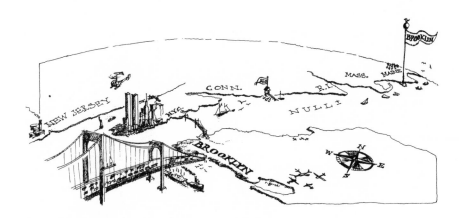

CHAPTER 18

The Order of Wholly Wooden Boat Owners

IF YOU'RE LIKE most of us wooden boat owners you've probably read more than you care to know about buying one. I blush to say that in my past I have taken money to write such articles. But no one has yet written helpfully on how to own one. I don't mean how to maintain one; everyone knows *that* can't be done. I mean how to endure, cope with, tolerate, the heady mixture of awe and contempt with which other people you know, the sensible ones, react to your boat. "Boy," they say, "you really must be dedicated," as if you have just entered an austere order of holy friars or taken a vow of poverty. In effect, of course, you have done just that; but how tacky of others to imply it. Or, "Gosh, can you really go to sea in that?", as if your boat had been built by a Japanese master of the art of decorative paper-folding. Now, having recently moved self and family aboard the 61-year-old, gaff-rigged English cutter CONTENT, I have experienced not only the wooden boat reaction syndrome but also the reaction to the *antique* wooden boat. That's like dandruff *and* mange.

It started even before we got away from the mooring in the upper Chesapeake where we took possession of the old girl. The folks at the marina, where I had stopped to buy hard tack and salt horse, admired CONTENT; but the admiration had something of the quality of the American tourist's admiration for the Pyramid of Khufu—magnificent, but now let's go see something else.

The manner of our departure did little to erase this attitude of admiring condescension. I started our 1926, three-cylinder Lathrop with a mighty heave on the lever with which one cranked its lethal, cast-iron flywheel. We cast off the mooring and instantly lost all power to our 27-inch, two-bladed propeller. Gearbox ailment.

One of our company had the foresight to have been employed formerly as ship captain for a certain Cunard company. Our good friend Captain Hunt is one of those men at whose left hand sit whatever gods of internal combustion may exist. We were glad to have him along. My own talent with machinery stops somewhat this side of the wheelbarrow. The gearbox fixed, off we chugged in a flat calm, down the Sassafras River bound for Chesapeake City on the C and D Canal.

We got there late that night. It would have been early that night, but I didn't recognize it when I got there. I thought it would look like a city. What it looked like was a gas dock. If the chart had said Chesapeake Gas Dock, why, I'd have got there right spang off. As it was, I was up-tide of the only available space along the seawall, having run by the metropolis.

Here I encountered another dimension in *owning*, rather than merely *buying*, a wooden boat, in my case owning a large and antique wooden boat with an 11-foot widow-maker jutting forward of the stem, almost horizontal to the waterline. When you're steaming toward a landing people ashore tend to get fidgety. Poor old CONTENT seems to unhinge the less stable ones altogether. Through the entire landing procedure, though, you are not allowed to show more concern than an occasional intestinal spasm.

We got ourselves tied up despite all the help, and at last Captain Hunt emerged from the swelter of the engine room, aptly dubbed the "hell hole," where he had been marinating almost continually during our passage. The old Lathrop ran, you see, at a temperature of practical use mainly to high energy atomic physicists. A man whom we had chugged right past several hours previously came over to examine us with the curiosity of an entomologist who has just discovered a rather large and unfamiliar type of beetle. At 700 rpm we had churned by him without a ripple, while his 1800 rpm roared in disbelief.

"May I see your power?" he asked. Captain Hunt slid back the hatch. The man stared silently at what appeared to be the terminal end of a pipe through which an automotive supply warehouse had been extruded ungently.

"Boy," he said, "I sure wish I had your engine."

"Sir," said Captain Hunt, "so do I."

Then Captain Hunt began to laugh. He laughed for a long time—a very long time. In time, I think he'll be his old self again.

CHAPTER 19

Daysail CONTENT?

WHEN WE BOUGHT old CONTENT some two years ago, the departing owner remarked that "You can't daysail her," meaning that it was just too much of a muchness to get her 20 plus tonnage and her copious rigging ready to sail if one were going to return the same day. His remark would seem even more true in that we have since removed her engine. Well, this report is to attest that you jolly well can daysail her. All it takes is a certain inner resource of native stupidity seasoned with the dogged, bull-headed perseverance of the medieval Bulgarian peasant.

We had invited friends to join us for a day's sail on Long Island Sound and I had decided to sneak the old hooker out of the slip before the falling tide caught her, and wait for our guests out in the channel, where there was plenty of water even at low tide. I glanced at the tide table and saw that if I hurried I could just make it and that even if I grounded she would float off in about an hour—plenty of time for my guests to come aboard, stow their gear, and have breakfast. Unfortunately, I began my maneuvering before waking my good seawife. That's important because she is the one who knows how to read a tide table and also knows the difference between standard and daylight time. I use *Eldredge's* tables, which repeat the warning to add an hour for daylight time on each page and in bold faced type. Obviously that is inadequate and I hereby put the editors on notice to beef up that warning so as to make it more noticeable. Perhaps something utilizing white phosphorus . . . but I digress.

The result of this misreading was that I had neatly caught the tide not just after low water but just before it, so now had to sit on the mud trying to look nonchalant while worrying about how much she'd heel. At this point we discovered that the cat, with that higher wisdom of his kind, had jumped ship. I got into the dinghy and called to the dog to jump in before I motored slowly back to the slip, some 100 feet away. Why the dog? The cat loves the dog and will almost always appear from hiding when the dog is about. (The attentive reader will have noted that though we have no engine we do have a cat and a dog—a clue to our priorities.) Now, picture this vignette: A large gaff-rigged cutter is aground in the channel of a busy harbor. The skipper, apparently unconcerned about his vessel, has gotten into his dinghy with a large dog and is put-putting slowly along the piers, calling out "Here, kitty-kitty-kitty," in that ridiculous falsetto that people always use when calling cats, though it never works. The cat did appear, though, when it saw the dog, and I returned to CONTENT.

When our guests arrived we were still aground, though the tide was rising. That raised the specter of coming off with no wind and no anchor out while close aboard rather expensive-looking yachts. So, back into the dinghy went I to get some lines across to a friend's boat that was tied up at the end of a nearby pier. I knew he wouldn't mind because he was away. Having done that, I asked everyone to get as far forward as possible, while I danced the jig at the end of the bowsprit, hoping to raise her stern enough to get her off. Nothing. Another friend offered to try towing us off but that too failed when our towline broke. We tried again, this time fouling the line in his propeller. He freed it. Finally, another jig on the bowsprit, and off we came to the cheers of the multitude.

Off we went, cat, dog, people, lines, and picnic gear strewn about the decks, happy to be on our way and that it was only mid-afternoon. Off came the mains'l stops. I slacked the port topping lift, to make it easy to get the gaff between port and starboard topping lifts as we raised it.

We hauled away at the peak and throat halyards and sweated them home, then the same for the stays'l and yankee halyards. Then we coiled all four halyards, flemishing the peak and throat. We signaled our good friend to drop the towline and hauled it aboard as we fell off on starboard tack. We slacked away the port forward and after running backstays, sheeted in the yankee, stays'l, and main, hauled the 45-pound plow anchor into the bow roller (I always let it hang just below the bobstay until in open water, just in case I need it fast), flaked down the 40 feet of anchor chain, and slacked away both topping lifts—and that's all there is to getting CONTENT away on a tack.

After we'd done all that, we were getting too close to Long Island for comfort and it was time to come about and run home, anyway. We had a fine run home and I got a chance to catch my breath for damn near five minutes before it was time to run the tack of the yankee inboard (it travels on the bowsprit by a hoop), lower away, get in the yankee stops, ease the plow down to the bobstay, flake out the throat and peak halyards, drop the peak a bit, slack off both leeward running backstays, set up the windward ones, hang the mains'l stops along the boom, drop the stays'l, round up in the outer mooring basin, drop the hook, lower the main, furl it, stop it, coil the main sheet, set up both topping lifts, winch up the hook, raise the stays'l, sail to about 30 feet to windward of the slip, drop the stern anchor, drop the bow anchor, take bow, stern and spring lines to the pier, pick up the stern and bow anchors, warp the old barn into the slip stern to, hook up the telephone and electricity, and have a drink.

In the evening, we sat in the cozy main cabin, ate a delicious meal made more so by our exertions and camaraderie and watched the sun go down over the Sound. We had much laughter about things that, considered out of the context of that day and outside old CONTENT's warm teak cabin, probably wouldn't seem so amusing.

Daysail CONTENT? It was worth it in spades—and that doesn't make any sense at all.

CHAPTER 20

"Performance" in the Gaff and Baggywrinkle Set

LIKE MANY of my colleagues among the gaff and baggywrinkle set, I have long affected a snooty disdain for shallow-minded sailors who are preoccupied with something the advertisements call "performance." I won't single these base fellows out by name; they know who they are. They are all those people with faster boats than mine. Early in the season they don't get to me. That's because they're all in sheds burnishing their boats' bottoms with No. 8000 wet-dry production paper, goosedown grit. During that all-too-brief span, old CONTENT has the Sound virtually all to herself and my good seawife and I, looking up at CONTENT's gently billowing high-peaked gaff-headed main, her motionless forestays'l and gallant high-footed yankee jib, can enjoy the fleeting illusion that the old hooker is going fast. In fact, she *is* going fast, if speed in sailing craft is to a large extent a subjective phenomenon. Any way you slice it, six knots in a 20-knot breeze ain't bad.

Inevitably, though, it happens. Along about the middle of May, we'll be bowling along with a hatful of wind on the quarter, just the way she likes it, happy as a clam in Cuttyhunk. Then I'll hear the whispering hiss of another boat's bow wave behind me. It'll be some dentist from Westport in his Merrill Lynch 45, the one with the trim tabs for the trim tabs. Remember now, this is the guy and the boat whom I affect to hold in lofty disdain. Just one question. If I hold him in such lofty disdain, why do I suddenly think that my throat halyard isn't sweated hard enough? Why do I want Nancy to check the luffs of the heads'ls? Who said six knots wasn't so bad?

I force a false grin at him as he storms through my lee. (Why do they always have to go through my lee?) He returns my grin and says something like, "Beautiful boat," or "When was she built?" That's gracious of him, I know. It's his way of saying, "I'm sorry to humiliate you but my boat is just simply much faster than yours—but here's a little compliment for you, my good man." And so sunk in depravity am I, that I eagerly catch the thrown verbal sop, like a beagle in the great hall of some duke. In fact, if such sops are not thrown, I become cross and pout. Perhaps this reaction to being passed is a throwback to my younger days, when I had the sense to race small, fast boats. But I don't believe any of us, no matter how much we *say* we're only interested in "cruising" (i.e., sailing inattentively), can watch a boat of like waterline length sail through our lee and still maintain a sense of inner peace and brotherhood with all living things. Me—I'd like to pitch a beer can at the bastard.

Perhaps the old racing juices never really dried up. Perhaps they were rejuvenated by John and Edgar. John and Edgar came aboard as crew one day a few years back when I sailed in the Danish-American Friendship Race. (If I wanted you to know how I finished, I'd have told you.) John and Edgar were all over the boat before we got to the starting line, changing this lead, adjusting that vang (they actually rigged vangs!), changing heads'l sheet leads, and sweating up halyards as if the old girl had been a 12-meter. Then, when everything was to their satisfaction, they wrapped masking tape around the halyards and sheets to mark key positions for various effects they were after.

One of those pieces of tape yet remains on my throat halyard, as a silent reproach. That I haven't removed it is proof that those old juices are still down there—deep, but flowing. That's why my affectation of disdain for the Westport dentist *is* an affectation. Why else would I always grow tight-lipped when that damned piece of tape comes into sight as I horse on the throat halyard? I can get it to within about a foot of the pin rail before my tongue starts clinging to the roof of my mouth.

"That'll do," I croak and Nancy belays. But she can see the tape, too, and the 12 inches still to go. And we know that way deep—it will *not* do. Soon, a masthead Marconi speed merchant comes charging up astern. Ah, John and Edgar, where are you now that I need you? But this time, I'll show 'em. Nobody barges through Old Stormalong's lee.

"Ready about!" I cry, and then, "Let's have a beer while she's going 'round!"

CHAPTER 21

Navigation by the Surliness Index

I MADE THE same mistake the other day that I've made many times in the past. I started to read something in *Bowditch* that I thought I understood, only to realize after a few pages that I didn't understand it at all, that another bastion of secure knowledge had sloughed away in my dotage, as shingles depart their barn roofs during New England winters. At this rate of shrinkage, in a few years my knowledge will consist of "red right returning" and "port wine is red."

The *Bowditch* material that has left me so shaken covers the relationship between time and longitude. I thought the matter was simple. There's Greenwich Mean Time, which is wrong, and Local Mean Time, which is correct. The farther west you go, the more wrong GMT gets. But alas, it's much more complicated than that. The trouble seems to be that the people in Greenwich think their clocks are right. In addition, something funny's going on at the international dateline. There's a force or heaven-knows-what out there that makes you look at the wrong day in the Nautical Almanac if you get too close. Hell, I thought all I had to worry about was dry rot and shipworms.

Anyway, I have simply decided to leave the entire matter of time and longitude theory to the experts and to depend on my own methods of finding longitude, which have never failed me. The surest method is to go ashore and ask someone where you are. Then you can look at your chart and find the corresponding longitude. That's embarrassing, though, so I have devised another method. That method is based on the close relationship between longitude of the vessel and surliness of dockmasters and fuel dock personnel along the northeastern coast of our nation. The closer you sail to New York City, the greater the surliness index, until maximum surl is encountered in waters between the Verrazano Narrows and Hell Gate.

If you were to leave from, say, Provincetown, where dockmasters and fuel personnel are downright friendly and helpful (a negative surliness index) and proceed down the coast toward New York City, you would be able to plot longitude as a function of decreasing negative surl (people may still treat you well but with a slight, although detectable, difference). Navigation in Massachusetts and

Rhode Island waters is difficult because the slope of the curve here is very gradual. For instance, people in Newport are damn near as nice as people in Woods Hole, but careful plotting (I can supply special plotting sheets) will locate the prudent mariner plus or minus 10 minutes of longitude. The slope of the surliness versus longitude curve begins to grow steeper as one goes west of New London. People are still pretty nice to old wooden gaffers, but one does begin to encounter the odd dockmaster who won't sell you five gallons of diesel on your credit card or who looks at you and your boat with the friendly warmth of a Croatian border guard.

As you proceed westward, the slope of the curve steepens until somewhere between New Haven and Larchmont there is a null point, a point where people are neither surly nor pleasant—something like a tidal node, where tidal range is zero and increases on either side. The precise spot is unknown to science, although I have written to the International Geodetic Society suggesting that a research project be funded for the next international geophysical year. It's probably at a place with a name like "Al's Bait and Tackle."

As a rough measure of longitude near the null zone, I offer the following tip: Anchor just off the fuel dock of a marina of unknown longitude. Dress in your grungiest clothing and row—do not motor—your dinghy ashore. Ask the man with the bill cap and wearing sunglasses if you can use the showers. Offer to pay the fee, if any. If he refuses permission and tells you that showers are for slip occupants only, you're west of Larchmont. Add 15 minutes of longitude if he calls you "Mac." If he says, "Why certainly—no charge," you're east of New Haven. Subtract 15 minutes of longitude if he praises your boat.

A note of caution: In the region of the null zone for surliness, anomalies exist—patches of decreased or increased surl density, much akin to magnetic anomalies that disturb patterns of compass variation. For instance, in Bridgeport, just inside the null zone, I once encountered a marina operator who not only remained patient and cooperative while trying to direct me to his deepest dock as I repeatedly ran CONTENT's eight-foot draft into the muck, but who opened up his store after hours just because I needed supplies, and then invited my wife and me to share his family's evening meal. So pleasant was he that I thought I was well east of Stonington. I have reported him to the Coast Guard as a navigational hazard but so far the *Notice to Mariners* supplements remain silent on the matter. I advise all prudent mariners to mark their charts accordingly.

CHAPTER 22

Courtesy Afloat

COURTESY AFLOAT—who but some congenital weirdo-nonconformist would object to courtesy afloat? You guessed it, you clever rascal you; I would. Courtesy afloat is as over-rated as ratchet screwdrivers and any motion picture with subtitles. Oh sure, there are times when a friendly word here and there may not do outright harm, but such deviations from a norm of grumpy reticence should be looked upon with grave suspicion. After all, when a chap says, "Good morning," as you cross his track, any sensible sailor has to wonder what the bastard is after. That can start off with a grim sequence of thoughts that can only be avoided by firing back, "Good morning," before one's adversary is out of earshot, giving him something to worry about, too. It's called counterpunching.

Courtesy when combined with helpfulness can be a real threat. In this regard, the United States Coast Guard is especially adept. Aboard CONTENT, we have unusually intimate experience with the devastating effect of USCG mastery of the courteous-helpful attack. Our extra experience stems from CONTENT's sailing qualities, excellent off soundings, but for close work she's about as handy as a gravel barge, although not as close winded. Consequently, we have had a number of conversations with the gentlemen and women of the Coast Guard, all of whom, I am sorry to report, employ the courteous-helpful attack.

Here's how it works. We had been sailing through dense fog all morning and part of the afternoon, looking for Block Island. This is an extremely difficult landfall because someone keeps moving it. Nevertheless, our spirits were high and we were all confident of making a good landfall because of the skipper's careful dead reckoning. In fact, so thoroughgoing had been my approach to pilotage on this occasion that I actually had the chart out and had already written several numbers on it.

Then it happened. The fog began lighting up all around us in periodic pulses of blue light—a strobe. Now, I don't know about you, but as soon as I am exposed to a strobe light either ashore or afloat my reflex reaction is, "Oh God, what have I done wrong, this time?"

Add to this the element of terror, for we couldn't tell yet where the light was coming from, and you have a heady mixture of emotions, indeed. Are we to be inspected by 18-year-old fugitives from the Pantry Pride checkout counter or run down by the TOYOTA MARU?

Soon the ambiguity began to resolve itself as we charged along with every rag set. (Yes, in Block Island Sound you can have wind *and* fog.) Through the fog we could just barely discern a little knot of small boats clustered around a Coast Guard cutter, the source of the strobe light.

Remember, all was well aboard old CONTENT; no one was uptight about anything. As we passed a few hundred feet away, a bull-horn-amplified, courteous-helpful voice boomed across the water, "Sir, are you disoriented?"

Disoriented? How the hell was I to answer? I hadn't *thought* I was disoriented until the question was posed, but perhaps I *should* have been disoriented. After all, there was the USCG cutter looking official, efficient, and vaguely menacing, surrounded by these little boats that sure as hell looked disoriented to me. In fact, they reminded me of kittens or puppies milling around the large body of their mama. I'm sure I saw a cute little Cal-24 try to suckle, but it was gently fended away. Perhaps any proper seaman would have been disoriented. Why would mother Coast Guard ask me if there hadn't been good, probable cause? Perhaps my failure to be disoriented was a mark of my own ineptitude.

These were my thoughts on hearing the Coast Guard's masterfully destructive question. I could have replied, "No, that is, I didn't think so until you asked, but are you implying that I should be? If so, I'd be happy to become disoriented if in fact I am not already in that state without realizing it," but it is extremely difficult to yell something like that. I mean, it's hardly, "Where away!?" or "Avast there!" is it? What I yelled was, "Well, if Block Island bears 110 degrees magnetic, I'm not disoriented. If it doesn't, I am."

The Coast Guard yelled back, "You're in the right ball park, sir."

So we sailed on, shaken, but grateful for having found out that it was OK not to have been disoriented. But note the effect of that deft little question by the Coast Guard. We were instantly transformed from comfortable, contented sailors into self-questioning, insecure neurotics, victims of courtesy afloat.

Our troubles were not to be over so simply, however. We soon saw the outer channel marker into Block Island's Great Salt Pond, lowered our sails, and began motoring in. Behind us, in the fog, we could hear the rumble of the Coast Guard's big diesels. Soon we could see them, big mama followed by her brood of small boats. Politely, courteously, the Coast Guard was waiting for us to negotiate the very narrow channel before bringing her brood through. In other words, we were holding everybody up as we cautiously picked our way along in the fog. Any decent chap would have roared around us in a great cloud of hydrocarbons, leaving us rolling in his wake and giving us a chance to vent our spleen about "those damned powerboats." But no, this Coast Guard skipper was lying back there, putting this big guilt trip on us for holding everyone up. So there we were, having been made to feel inadequate *and* guilty, all in the space of one afternoon by one courteous and helpful Coast Guard skipper.

Soon we were through the channel and into the pond itself. No sooner had we got our hook down when a powerboat zoomed out of the fog so close across our bow that I thought he would cut our anchor chain. It was good to be back where at least some people know how to behave on the water.

CHAPTER 23

An Alien Afloat

S OMEDAY I WILL make a great deal of money by writing a book about how to go to marinas. I will do this as soon as I find out how it's done. I know, it sounds easy—just go. But it's not easy. It's hard, because the world of marinas is very different from the world in which old CONTENT is usually to be found. CONTENT is an alien in the world of marinas, an alien without her "green card."

CONTENT's world is a working boatyard. It's filled with the sounds of high-speed drills, air compressors, pumps, and diesel engines, and it's populated by people wearing funny suits and spraying things on boats while other people in funny suits scrape off the stuff the first people sprayed on three years ago. CONTENT is at home here, in all senses of the word, because work has always been part of her heritage.

Perhaps that is why she and marinas don't seem to get along. Marinas are part of the world of playtime—and rich people's playtime, at that. Marinas are filled with the sounds of radios (usually housed in automobiles designed to look like spaceships or suppositories), loud hailers, and burbling gasoline engines (usually in boats designed to look like cars), and are populated by people wearing noisy red Bermuda shorts. Marinas give off a smell of mingling diesel fuel, gasoline, and suntan oil.

As soon as I begin to approach the fuel dock of such an establishment, I begin to feel—this is the only word for it—inappropriate. It's as if a working man in bib overalls were approaching the front gate of a Monte Carlo casino. Not that we are often rebuffed; quite the contrary, we are usually—well—tolerated. But I still *feel* as if I am in bib overalls.

The first difficulty in fact is that CONTENT is well tolerated—too well, as far as certain physical constraints are concerned. The first chapter in my "How to" book is going to be called, "Whaddya Mean, 'Plenty of Water'?!" You see, CONTENT has been aground more often at fuel docks than are some pilings during northern winters. My first chapter will explain that dockmasters habitually either overestimate the depth of water at their docks or report it with the vagueness of a political party's position paper in an election year. How many feet are there in "plenty," anyway?

Then there's the matter of dockside help. I don't know which is worse: trying with assistance to get CONTENT alongside and in between two yachts owned by Venezuelans with no visible means of support, or maneuvering without someone ashore to take lines. Theoretically, of course, it's nice to have someone ashore, but that was more true in the old days when that someone was probably named Al, chewed Red Man, said "Yep" and "Nope" a lot, and wore steel-toed shoes.

Today, the fellow ashore is articulate, calls you "Cap," and wears Gucci sandals. His name is probably Chuck or Chip, and he knows as much about what to do with a bow line as my cat knows about the Hanseatic League. He's likely to just stand there or, even worse, begin to shamble forward with it. To the question, "What do you want me to do with it, Cap?" there is only one answer, but it's too obvious to actually say it.

Only once did I actually see poetic justice done. I guess CONTENT herself couldn't resist the temptation. CONTENT had just come alongside a fuel dock and was still ranging forward at a good clip. This time, though, I had room to stop her with the engine, so I yelled to the chap ashore to go forward and just make the bow line fast. But, as it happened, *this* fellow was a female, probably named Melanie. She was dressed just like Chuck or Chip. Not heeding my yell and girlishly anxious to show off her agility and enthusiasm, she hurled all 105 pounds against the line and tried to stop CONTENT's forward motion. Even though I already had fully reversed, she was pulled right off her Guccis.

CONTENT was just the wrong boat for that marina. Melanie might have been stopping boats that way for years, but surely they were different boats— lighter displacement, bigger engines, more easily maneuvered. In fact, when Melanie got to her feet she was put out with me for not going astern. When I explained that I had been going astern for quite some time, she said, "Gosh, what kind of boat is that, anyway?"

I told her all about CONTENT, but what I should have said was that she was right to be put out with me. I had been going astern, certainly, but I should never have been there in the first place.

It's not that I have anything against women as dockhands (well, in fact I do, but that's another matter); it's more that the presence of a female dockhand in halter, shorts, funny shoes, and looking like a Melanie should have warned me that this was the wrong place for bib overalls and steel-toed shoes. I should have looked for a dock with shrimp boats tied up. Trouble is, CONTENT doesn't really belong there, either—not really. She is, after all, *not* a working boat.

And commercial docks seldom have floating piers; it's always low tide, and the enormous bollards are 10 feet over the deck. Even if we could get ashore there'd be no one around, because no one is ever around when we try to tie up at commercial docks. Everyone's at Joey's Diesel, getting a new fuel pump.

Maybe I should get a pair of red Bermuda shorts and try to pass CONTENT off as a Cal-40. Then I could feel at home at posh marinas. Gosh, come to think of it . . . that's a lousy idea.

CHAPTER 24

Fatigue Avoidance

NOBODY ASKED ME, but books and articles on safety afloat generally have it all wrong. Safety is not a matter of fire extinguishers, flotation gear, or lifelines and the like. Safety lies in the ability to sleep while others are either snoring or emitting other animal noises (sometimes with great enthusiasm). The great enemy of safety afloat is fatigue, for fatigue is the mother of apathy—and, in turn, the mother of dragged anchors, sprained ankles, and shattered interpersonal relationships.

The next time some crewmember is sleeping on the foredeck while the rest of you are scurrying about squinting at luffs and yelling, resist that impulse to rouse him with rude criticism. He may well be practicing that golden rule of safety at sea: fatigue avoidance. Ten hours from now, he may be the only rested person on the boat, while the rest of you eager beavers are lolling glassy-eyed in the lee bunks. It may be he and only he who, wide awake at the helm, is alert enough to notice that the jib mitre is beginning to tear. Manfully, he puts aside his cold can of Chef Boyar-dee ravioli and yells, "On deck, you bastards! Get that jib down before we lose it!"

You all tumble up on deck just in time to see the shreds disappearing into the gloom, bound for better weather. If you're lucky, you may even be treated to the sight of a shipmate falling through the open foredeck hatch, doubtless left open by the ravioli-lover. But hey, hunger makes fatigue even worse. Our safety-conscious gourmet was just trying to be extra careful.

If there's anything worse than fatigue, it's fatigue plus hunger. That combination can even act like a potent hallucinogenic drug. My personal style of hallucinating from fatigue and hunger, especially in fog, is to feel the boat yaw wildly off course despite my death grip on the tiller. This impression can make one "correct" involuntarily, so that when one does look at the compass the boat is yawing in a nautical example of the infamous "self-fulfilling prophecy." Because CONTENT likes to take her time about answering the helm (not enough for brewing a pot of coffee, though; that's a lie spread by my enemies), and because her compass card, like everything else about her, is slow, one can find oneself in a kind of mad tiller dance as one tries to correct course changes that are several days old, if indeed they ever occurred at all.

Fatigue, hunger, and fog can also produce weird distortions in depth perception. At least, that is my official line when explaining my failure to find Nantucket one late afternoon in August when the fog had just begun to roll in. As all New England sailors know, Nantucket is an unusual island in that it is actually floating, moored to an enormous mushroom anchor that allows it to change position according to variations in wind and tide. For this reason, it is quite rare to encounter the island on the same bearing from a given spot twice in a row. Imagine my surprise, then, when on the day in question it began to loom out of the murk precisely on the expected bearing.

Of course, I immediately realized that something was wrong. Because of my fatigue and hunger, I suddenly had the illusion that instead of looking at Nantucket light tower, a huge structure some five miles away, I was looking at a much smaller structure only a few dozen yards away. That's when the mad tiller dance began.

"Hard to port," I yelled.

"What in hell for?" responded my good seawife.

"Hard to starboard," I shouted, fine-tuning the command.

"Are you nuts?" she said, cutting right to the heart of the matter.

"It's not the light tower," I shrieked in a charming falsetto, and ran full tilt into the mast. Fatigue, you see, had claimed another victim. In my panic, I had forgotten where the mast was, and I've only got one. Can you imagine the lumps I would have taken by this time if I had been the owner of a three-masted schooner?

I believe that fatigue has tempted many sailors to commit one of the most dangerous among all errors in seamanship: trying to enter a harbor at night, when heaving-to or standing off would have been more prudent. Daylight makes things a lot clearer, even if you don't know where you are.

On that August afternoon when I forgot where my mast was, I at least had enough residual sense to drop the hook and wait out the fog. When morning came, I was able to get things sorted out and make a good passage down the channel into Nantucket Harbor. Strangely, some eccentric New Englander had put up a sign on the roof of his spar shed identifying the place as "Edgartown," but New England quirkishness is not the subject of this monograph.

Despite all the mishaps, I'd love to get back to New England one day—but not before they shorten up the scope on the Nantucket mooring line.

CHAPTER 25

The 20-Minute Workout

S AILING A BIG boat like that shorthanded must be pretty stren-
uous," my dinghy-sailing friend remarked.

Without a trace of shame, I replied that it was, indeed,
quite taxing at times. Actually, the average physical energy output
necessary to sail CONTENT is somewhat greater than what is required
to affix postage stamps but less than that necessary to pit olives. Of
course, there are moments when bursts of energy are needed, as
when raising the gaff or running out on the bowsprit in order to dis-
engage it from the telephone booth at the end of the fuel dock. Such
energy bursts are, of course, exactly what is *not* needed for physical
conditioning. They are, however, admirably suited for maintaining
the local medical and chiropractic communities in the lifestyles to
which they have become accustomed.

These experts tell us that we should not exercise when we are
tired and that we should always limber up first. Wonderful. When I
remember the times I've really had to hustle on CONTENT, it seems
they were also times when I was extremely tired and when I had had
about as much time to warm up as a pheasant flushed by a backhoe.

Any sailboat, but especially a big, old, ungainly gaffer like CON-
TENT, seems designed to provide ample opportunities for exactly the
wrong kind of exercise. Imagine being awakened from a sound sleep,
having cold water dashed in your face, and then having to do upper-
body calisthenics while some sadistic maniac tilts the room this way
and that. That's the equivalent exercise for getting rolled out of the
bunk in the wee hours and having to get a torn headsail down during a sudden squall. You can practice this exercise in the privacy of
your home. All it takes is a wet bedsheet, a powerful fan, and an assistant with a garden hose. The advanced student can enhance the
conditioning by having the assistant bellow incoherently at him
(incoherent except for the words, "Goddamn lee shore!").

For those romantic and exciting times when it is necessary to
raise the gaff, try this warmer-upper. Reach up and grab the top of a
door frame or other improvised "chinning" bar. Pull down. If your
feet come off the floor, you are not doing the exercise correctly. The

idea is to bring the bar down to you, not raise yourself up to the bar. Done properly, the warm-up accurately prepares you for raising the gaff because no gaff within the memory of man has ever gone up without the halyards fouling on something. Clearing halyards is generally a matter of correct word choice. The seasoned sailor knows how to imply a canine identity to the halyards' parents, impugn the sexual behavior of the halyards, and to combine these epithets in such a way that not only the halyards themselves but the halyards' mother is slandered. Note: Sometimes these verbal measures are so effective that the halyards suddenly clear themselves. To condition your rear for the resultant high-velocity impact with the deck, have your assistant whack you in the butt with a plank (either marine hardwood or exterior-grade plywood, depending on type of deck).

And, let's not forget our conditioning for those activities that require a kind of staying power, a combination of mental and physical stamina unique to sailors. Anyone who has ever stood an eight-hour watch (four-hour watches are a snare and a delusion—just try it sometime) on a moonless night with no stars and only the red binnacle light to show his course, knows what I mean. Keeping one's sanity is not the real issue; most wooden boat sailors are bonkers to begin with. How do you keep your butt from going numb? Ah, that is the question.

The answer is that you don't. Why do you think sailors often stand with their hands in their back pockets? They're reassuring themselves that their butts have not fallen off during the night. Getting used to long hours of doing nothing and yet paying close attention to the course is not easy, but there are warm-up exercises even for that.

For instance, watch ice form in the harbor if you're up North. I don't mean check it every few hours. Sit there and watch it every second. See how the crystals form and gradually coalesce. Really watch the damned ice form. In summer, watch the tide come in. Same thing; really watch as grain by grain of sand is covered. It's boring as hell—great mental training for standing a long watch alone. Note: Readers from the Bay of Fundy may skip this exercise. They have plenty of trouble already.

CHAPTER 26

The Check Is in the Mail

A S A PUBLIC service, I now list some statements that every sailor may expect to encounter many times during his or her seagoing career, statements that are never true. Knowing that they are never true won't do anyone a particle of good but may avoid psychic pain and disappointment. It might even help save the blue whale. Personally, I don't care. The statements are the nautical equivalent of, "The check is in the mail."

There's plenty of water over there.
This statement is characteristic of someone who *wishes* there were plenty of water over there, wherever "there" happens to be. The speaker really means, "If there were plenty of water over there, you would dock at my marina" (or restaurant, bar, etc., or even that you would get the hell away from the fuel dock so that a real big spender could tie up). It is a fundamental law of nature that no one who has ever assured the skipper that there was plenty of water over "there" has ever first asked about the draft of one's boat. Just remember that there is a crucial difference between you and anyone else you're likely to ask about sufficient depth of water over "there." You are aboard your boat; the other person is not. Six hours from now, he will be going on about his business (of course, you ran aground at high tide); you will be screaming at your loved ones and shattering lifelong friendships while still trying to lasso a dock piling.

We'll weigh anchor at first light.
You most certainly will do no such thing. Even in the unlikely event that you or someone wakes up at first light, it will take at least two more hours before you are even ready to attempt to weigh anchor. The reasons for this are legion, but the top-ranked ones are: (1) Herbie and Edna took the dinghy to shore at 0500 in order to find a loaf of bread and aren't back yet, having been unable to find their way back to the boat, and (2) Herbie and Edna have taken the dinghy to shore but have been unable to find the shore. Not to worry, they will be back in the fullness of time, as soon as the morning fog lifts, in

71

tow by the harbor police who have cited them for no life jackets and who will now cite you for registration numbers that are below the minimum size mandated by the Treaty of Ghent. Only after the coppers have finished their inspection of your boat and called you "Sir" 73 times in a tone of voice that turns your insides to haggis will you be free to weigh anchor. Even that will take hours, because the anchor's snagged under the continental shelf and freeing it will entail removal of a significant portion of Rhode Island (not in itself a bad idea). This brings us to . . .

It'll burn off by ten.

Even if the aforementioned were not the case, you would not have weighed the anchor at first light, because at first light the visibility was no greater than 17 centimeters. Predictions about "burning off" (whatever that's supposed to mean) are generally made by people who haven't the faintest conception of the phenomenon they think they are describing. These are the same people who talk about "crystallization" in connection with metal fatigue and who routinely suggest more inside ballast to stiffen a tender boat. In all of recorded history, no fog within 2,000 miles of Pollock Rip has ever dissipated until at least one hour after the time specified by any given self-appointed old Capt. Stormalong. Indeed, one famous fog off Kennebunkport persisted throughout an entire presidential term, lifting only with the onset of a Democratic administration. Doubters are referred to the archives of the American Meteorologic Society. Fogbound sailors may be tempted to emit the next eternally untrue statement.

There is a spare flashlight in the lazarette.

There *used* to be a spare flashlight in the lazarette. You've been using the spare for weeks, ever since you dropped the good police-sized rubberized one overboard. You have been meaning to get another high-quality flashlight to replace it, but, like reading *War and Peace*, you haven't gotten around to it yet. Even if you had a spare flashlight, it wouldn't be in the lazarette. It would be . . . somewhere else . . . not discoverable until at least three days after the day you really needed it.

We should see the whistle buoy in a half-hour.

Strictly speaking, this statement is true; you should see it in that time if only the world were a perfect place. If only you were where you think you are, going where you think you're going, and if the buoy were where it is supposed to be. Since these conditions are never true simultaneously, the statement is never true. Note that since you are looking for a whistle buoy, conditions may be such that one expects to hear it before one sees it. In that case, one must be cautioned against steering in the direction of the sound. That is because whistle buoys have a perverse and cruel sense of humor and have been known to change their position as soon as anyone starts trying to find them. Just hold your course and act nonchalant. In a worst-case scenario you should consider anchoring and sending Herbie and Edna out to look for it. With any luck, you might lose them this time.

PART THREE

Keeping
CONTENT

CHAPTER 27

A Heavy Moral Burden

SPRING IS COMING and with it a heavy moral burden. It begins to weigh upon me already, even though the ice is still four-inch thick around CONTENT's protective copper sheathing. Though sustained by a hot mug of cocoa and a cheery crackling TV, I feel the heavy hand of duty already upon my drooping shoulder. Soon it will be spring and I will have to make the old girl ready to sail again. It's either that or finish the job begun last December when I made her ready for winter. I've already got the bloody rafters over the boom and her keel is deep in the mud these winter ebb tides. How much more trouble would it be to tack tarpaper over the rafters, shingles over that, and cement-block the old hooker to the bottom on the next ebb?

But no, there's the moral burden. After all, how would it look? Owning an old classic boat is like owning a $200 pool cue in a custom-made teak and velvet carrying case. If you do, you'd better be a damned serious pool player. CONTENT has forced us to live up to her in a similar way. We certainly have to sail her early in the season and keep at it until the next winter's snow falls. It's expected, you see. Why, we even drew sneers aplenty when we got the TV. Now, if we had lived aboard a reverse sheer, polywhatsit electromat, we could have had a color set and not gotten flak.

It wouldn't be so heartrending if all I had to face was the standard masochistic ritual with which we all respond to the vernal equinox. But that's only the beginning for me. The combination of winterizing the boat and living aboard has turned her into something that would pass for an aftermath of a tornado that's swept through a chandlery, a cordage mill, supermarket, and Al's Army Surplus.

Last December, just for one example, I unreeved all my halyards to prevent chafing during those three-day blows of winter. As I worked, a friend jested, "Better take notes." Not two days ago, as I gazed up through the skylights at the immense coils of line that were my peak and throat halyards and contemplated the rerigging job a thought slowly began to form behind my Neanderthal eyebrow ridges. "Gee," went the thought, "I should have taken notes."

I'm pretty sure I could figure it out if I could just have the teensiest hint. I've been looking at old snapshots of CONTENT under sail with something more than mere esthetic interest but they have been of general help only and I'm ashamed to go around the docks asking friends if they have any old snapshots of her under sail. How would I explain my keen interest?

Then there's the gaff. I've completed the repair following last year's annual gaff-breaking but now I have to put back all the attaching parts. On the gaff they didn't look like much and their functions were self explanatory but staring at me from inside the plastic bag that now houses them, they seem mysterious indeed. I suppose I could try to complete the job at night but I'm not sure I could finish by morning. How would it look for me to be discovered at sunrise—bonkers?

Then, there's the matter of what remains of my winter cover. I mean the part that stayed behind when the rest was last seen making about 50 knots, 350 degrees true at 0400 some months ago—going before the wind of course. That carnage has to be cleared away. Then there's the cockpit, glutted with sailbags, outboard engine, gas tank, and I hope the missing silverware.

It's hard to believe that this seagoing version of Tobacco Road will ever be a boat again, but of course it will. We'll get it done—the moral burden, you know. But after all of that, the real travail lies in wait—the testing of our inner fiber.

This spring CONTENT is to have her diesel. Now, putting the diesel in is not the test I'm talking about. That merely entails ripping out our double bunk that cost me an average of $2.50 per board foot and demolishing the cockpit and ripping out the cabin sole and disrupting our lives for a few weeks. No, the real trial will not be in *installing* the diesel, it will be in *having* the diesel.

You see, until the coming of the diesel I will have gotten one hell of a lot of undeserved credit for being "the guy who maneuvers that big old cutter in and out with no engine." The credit is undeserved because warping with docklines, kedging, etc., takes a lot more mulishly stolid resolve and determination than it does finesse. Hell, you don't get going fast enough to hurt anything. And if one does muck it up a bit, scrape a rail here, tap a bowsprit there, why everyone is extremely forgiving—"no engine, you know."

I've been like a man playing the clarinet while wearing mittens. It would require a tremendous amount of mistakes before that man drew hisses and catcalls. But let him take those cowardly mittens off—now, let's see how the swab plays.

I've been sailing so long without an engine that the thought of being able to stop the boat and actually to back her fills me with dread. You see, if one *can* do that with a boat, one *must* do it. There's your moral burden again. Gone are the days—or soon will be—when I could shrug at the dockmaster who wanted me to shoehorn the old girl into a space that would leave her bowsprit jutting over $4,000 worth of fighting chairs, deep sea fishing reels, poles, outriggers, Loran, Decca, Chivas Regal, and a nervous chubby realtor in red Bermuda shorts. Gone will be those days when I could yell "no engine, can I tie up at the gas dock for a minute?"

Soon, I shall have to try to snake her into that terribly tight spot. The chubby realtor will glare balefully at my bowsprit and the dockmaster will shout wrong advice with a tone of salty assurance. I will hate both of them before the bow line has gone ashore.

An idea occurs to me. I could put on these mittens, see, and when the . . . no, forget it. One must shoulder one's moral burden . . . probably wouldn't work anyway.

CHAPTER 28

Bilge Treasures

SOME DEWY-EYED romantics are fond of flipping through old photograph albums or family scrapbooks in order to recall the past, but let me tell you that for evoking one's past, nothing can compare to cleaning out CONTENT's bilge. That's one of the overlooked disadvantages of your modern shallow-draft skimming dish boats—practically no bilge—a few old magazines, a bag of Fritos, a two-week supply of socks, and such a bilge is filled to the cabin sole. How in hell can you develop a sense of personal history with one of those short-memory bilges? Where would we be if, on opening the tomb of Tutankhamen, we had found nothing older than the August 1925 *National Geographic*?

On the other hand, CONTENT's bilge is copious enough to house untold years of the debris of our daily lives—a bilge to conjure with—a bilge large enough to have acquired the aura of wonder that has always been attached to the contemplation of the remote past. Our bilge bears the same relation to our past as do ancient archaeological digs to *Homo sapiens'* past. In fact, if I were to find a chipped flint or a mastodon femur in the bilge one day, it wouldn't surprise me a bit. I owned the boat for months before I discovered an ancient 40-gallon water tank down there, and I know there's a sizable 12-volt motor beneath the sole—somewhere; I can hear it running when I throw a certain switch.

My remembrance of things past was triggered recently when one of my bilge pumps became clogged and I was forced to excavate. I had been viewing the prospect with dread, not realizing then the fine sense of historical continuity I was about to gain. But no sooner had I picked up the floorboards when a great veil fell from my eyes.

My old pipe wrench! So that's what had been staining my bilge-water with rust all these years! I soon fell into a reverie. Let's see now—that old wrench (good old wrench!) first "went missing" back in '76, about a week after I had heard that "kersplash" while rolling at anchor in Duck Island Roads. Viewing the rusty pipe wrench brought back that entire cruise, the grateful sense of security that comes from being in the lee of a good breakwater, on good holding ground, while the gale blows itself out.

The bilge yielded up a treasure trove of mementos: pages from my long-lost Perkins diesel owner's manual, the hull of my son's model of the CUTTYSARK, the 1974 Cape May tide tables, courtesy of Angie's Bait and Tackle Shop, numerous crayons, my Argyle sock, and the remains of the shaving kit that Eastern Airlines gave me while they put a tracer on my baggage. And that's only what I got within arm's reach of where I was lying on the cabin sole. That's another nice thing about enormous bilges; there are still more goodies awaiting me up under the galley sole, the forepeak, the main cabin. They will rest in obscurity until another Force 8 duster in Block Island Sound sluices them down to the bilge pump, clogging it and forcing another archaeologic expedition.

Of course, the treasures of the bilge don't include only my tenure as CONTENT's skipper. Those treasures provide a link to my fellow man, her former skippers, who by all the evidence, seemed equally incapable of hanging onto their tools, papers, pens, and Argyle socks.

Certain tools that have belonged to past skippers entail a nasty, even spiteful, aura by their mere presence in the bilge. They're the most fun. I mean, a pipe wrench falls into the bilge and—big deal— there's no special implication. It might have fallen off an engine room shelf while no one needed it, as indeed had happened to my pipe wrench. If you did need it, it's not hard to fish out. But . . . a $\frac{3}{32}$-inch Allen wrench—Ah!—there's something else again. What a swearing and a moaning there must have been when *that* son of a bitch was dropped, for dropped it surely was; even sailors don't leave Allen wrenches lying around. They're either hung up or put away. No—an Allen wrench in a bilge means someone was using it when it fell out of his hand. And Allen wrenches are like Phillips screwdrivers and policemen: If you need one, you need it badly and substitutes just won't do.

I have found Allen wrenches and their ilk (very small open-end wrenches are another example, especially when found under engines) and delighted in thinking, "Now, you rotten little creep, you enraged one skipper but I've got you and I'm going to buff you up and oil you and put you in my tool box and you'll not do that to me, by Godfrey!" That's why I currently own two cheap plastic-handled wood chisels. They're pitted and probably never did hold an edge, but finding them right next to one another as I did, I feel sure that some spiritual shipmate of the past dropped one, cursed emphatically, reached for another and then dropped that one, too. He must have really been steamed! I owe it to him to keep those chisels.

Someday, the skipper that shall come after me will make a similar find and, I hope, think of me with similar misty sentimentality. In my case, I hope the artifact will be a 12-inch blue-and-white china plate. (I assume that the freshly-baked blueberry pie it once bore has long since been pumped into some ocean somewhere.) Pie, plate, and plastic bag disappeared one afternoon about two years ago. All were in the galley so they couldn't have gone overboard. Nancy and I searched diligently with flashlights, mirrors, and hands sore from tearing up floorboards, but could not find a trace.

I hope that skipper of the future, when he finds our plate (undoubtedly in some unbelievably unlikely cranny of the Bilge of Wonders) will think of our fretful puzzlement and use the plate with tenderness. I hope also that, as he thoughtfully fondles his new-found bilge treasure from the past, he doesn't notice his socket wrench extension rolling toward the edge of the bench. After all, the great wheel of history must continue to turn.

CHAPTER 29

Never Talk to Boat Carpenters

JUST AS I was beginning to think that I had learned at least the basic axioms of living aboard, I found that I still had a long way to go. I know, for instance, that if it were not for the charcoal briquette, half the liveaboard fraternity would starve to death; that the greatest human being who ever lived is the man who invented "Vise Grips"; that electrolysis is a process lying entirely outside the domain of the basic laws of the physical universe. But it was only recently that I learned something of even greater importance, something I had never before suspected: Never talk to boat carpenters. If a boat carpenter appears to want to talk to you, pretend that you are a Ukrainian tourist.

The reason is that boat carpenters arouse feelings of guilt every bit as effectively as do Jewish mothers. At least they do in me, and I think I can speak with some authority in this matter. There is a manifest similarity between "You mean you don't wash the dishes after each meal?" and "How come you didn't put wicking under each washer before tightening down the bolts?" Come to think of it, boat carpenters *are* Jewish mothers. The same compulsiveness about details, the same perfectionist striving for an ideal state, the same conviction that falling short of the ideal represents a kind of moral failure, characterizes each. For—make no mistake—when a boat carpenter criticizes the lack of wicking under a washer, he means not just that you've made a pragmatic error that may cause the bolt to "weep" sooner than otherwise, he means also that you've committed a moral crime, that you've been unethical.

I wouldn't find his attitude quite so hard to deal with if I could dismiss it as mindless fanaticism. What gravels my craw is the unspoken knowledge that the rotten bastard is right; it *is* a moral crime for me to let my decks leak, the rainwater run down my mast onto my mast step, to continue to ignore the telltale rust streak running down my stem from the stemhead casting. After all, most wooden boats will outlast any one owner. We have our charges in trust, so to speak, until we shuffle off to Fiddler's Green and another misguided numbskull stumbles into a boatyard one day, to pay off the liens. To let a fine wooden boat go to hell is a betrayal of future numbskulls and her departed builders.

I *know* that; and as I listen to the rain and watch the drops run down the deck beams, I have all the guilt I can handle. I don't need some young whippersnapping, granola-eating, Chapelle-quoting wood butcher to tell me with a mournful shake of the head that I "really ought to get after those decks." The trouble with such facile advice is that it ignores certain facts that characterize most real live-aboard families.

Living aboard is usually depicted as if the protagonists either are retired or are young adventurers with no children who can do whatever they want wherever they want. In fact, our main concern aboard old CONTENT is earning a living ashore, at a trade that has nothing to do with boats. Then come such nautical concerns as car insurance, taxes, groceries, and the effect of the prime rate on our quarterly payments. Decks? Yes, I must get after the decks, but the monkey dung that we are using costs $50 a gallon and my son needs new jeans, we're in arrears with the orthodontist bill, the repair work must take place right over where we eat dinner, do our homework, and knead the bread dough, and when I get home in the evening I'm ready for the slag heap, not deck planks.

The romantic liveaboard literature would have you believe that we could, say, careen the boat for bottom maintenance whenever we choose. As a veteran careener and liveaboarder, I can tell you that careening has as much to do with school and job schedules, public transportation and/or car logistics, the laws of trespass and private property rights as it does with tide tables and beach characteristics.

Those people in the magazines and books always seem completely detached from shore concerns, and so they may be. When they want to careen they careen; when they want to "get after those decks," they do so, but we who must toil in a less exalted vineyard must first see about the car insurance, get the braces adjusted, and find out why we have not yet heard from Frobisher and Freemish, Inc., about that check.

So, you see that when the boat carpenter admonishes us, however obliquely he goes about it, he is only aggravating an already festering wound. We have already admonished ourselves. The boat carpenter's comments are like admonitions to an alcoholic that he really ought to lay off the sauce, and they produce a similar reaction in the admonishee.

I know that this sounds like rationalization. I can almost hear the self righteous, "Pull yourself together, man; there's always the weekend to get after those decks!" And in fact we do *some* boat work on weekends, but man does not live by toil alone, and we have to go sailing *sometime*. Why else do we have the boat?

If it will make the boat carpenters happy, though, whenever I take old CONTENT out for a sail, my pleasure is tainted by the ever-present knowledge that I really should be back at the slip busting my gaboon over the decks. I'm really having a lousy time.

OK Mom?

CHAPTER 30

All Men Are Brothers

O
NE CLICHÉ about alcoholics is that they have to hit bottom
before they can begin to effect their own recovery—you
know, wake up in a sleazy doorway in some skid row, something like that. I don't know if that's really true of alcoholics, but I
know it's true of laggard wooden boat liveaboarders as far as boat
maintenance and repair are concerned. At least, it's true of *this* laggard, for I've just had the nautical equivalent of waking up in an
alley, reeking of muscatel, catching sight of myself in a broken mir-
ror, and saying to myself "Whoa there! Enough is enough; I gotta
turn it around!"

What I had to turn around was having not done any serious
maintenance on the old girl for about two years. As a full-time free-
lance writer, my income has been about on a par with that of a Welsh
coal miner in the 19th century—and I don't sing a tenth as well. So,
I haven't had the means to do right by the old girl, and when I have
gotten a few bucks ahead, I've been afraid to spend them. But all
that's changed, now that I've had that figurative doorway awakening.

It was like this. I was staring for the hundredth time, disconso-
lately, at the place where the hood ends of three planks have started
coming away from their landing on the stem. I was asking myself for
the hundredth time that most dreaded, most fearsome question
asked at one time or another by all owners of old wooden boats: "I
wonder what's going on under there?"

A young man festooned with cameras came over and said,
"Would you be interested in having your boat used in a movie?
We're looking for an old derelict like this." I thanked him but explained that it would require too much of a disruption in my seden-
tary and not a little crotchety lifestyle, then went below to sob into
my pillow. My dear old CONTENT OF FALMOUTH a derelict?!

I went topside again and walked a ways off to look at her. A lot
of that term "derelict" came from some superficial cosmetic characteristics, the old chain and spare anchors piled on deck, coils of line,
sailbags, and a circus tent affair suspended over the entire boat
against rain and sun. But chainplates were bleeding rust down the

sides, likewise the stemhead hardware, and of course there were those three damn planks. Even at her best, CONTENT puts one in mind of the AFRICAN QUEEN—she's that kind of boat—and if "derelict" was too harsh a term, certainly the old hooker was getting definitely funky. "Enough is enough," I cried, "I gotta turn it around!"

Without so much as a fearful glance at the checkbook, I strode resolutely to the boatyard sales office and ordered the first white oak I've ordered in two years. It was a watershed moment. I had embarked on what will probably be a three-year period of CONTENT restoration. True, the start was limited; merely the replacing of a cracked and suspiciously lumpy (I have been wondering for nine years what was going on there) carlin, or whatever the hell they call one of those short beams that go between the deckbeams under the skylight. Incidentally, having now finished taking out the old and installing the new beam, I can tell you what was, in fact, going on there. Just exactly what you think was going on there was going on there. When I finally got out the old piece, I had enough humus to mulch Julia Child's herb garden. Hell, I had enough to mulch Julia Child. It smelled like Sherwood Forest.

But, small as that beginning was, it was real. I'm on my way. I no longer have to look at other people in the yard carrying lumber, sweating, their hair blue, green, ochre (that damn ochre is about $50 a gallon; if I ever got any of that stuff on me I'd never wash it off), and think, gosh, I should really be doing something about CONTENT. The sound of power tools whining in the morning no longer fills me with guilty malaise. I, too, now make my own whining noises in the morning with the best of 'em, some of which noises come from *my* power tools. I feel righteous and smug. There is sawdust on my glasses and epoxy on my T-shirt.

My resurrection wasn't easy, though. When I placed my saw in contact with that 70-year-old oak I had more than a few qualms. My God, I was about to start sawing on a piece of ancient English oak that some old geezer, who had probably apprenticed for 10 years before they let him drive a nail unsupervised, had expertly placed there seven decades ago. Was I up to it? Would I—could I—do, as the English say, "a proper job"? And so, I gripped my saw—and began to cut. I half expected the old girl to scream as I sawed.

Soon, a wonderful thing happened. As I finally withdrew the old rotten carlin, which was let into the attaching deckbeams via mortise and tenon joints, there fell to the cabin sole, plunk, a shim! A shim, by the great Harry! The old geezer had cut the tenon a hair too short and, by Godfrey, had had to stuff a shim into a mortise to make the joint tight! "You were human after all, you bloomin' limey house carpenter!" I thought gleefully. "There'll be no shims in my joint!"

So I measured my new piece of oak with the care and precision of a neurosurgeon. I cut it with similar care. I also forgot to allow for the thickness of my saw when doing so, and my new beam was that much too short. I found an easy solution for the error, though. I won't tell you what I did. All I can say is that, indeed, all men are brothers.

CHAPTER 31

Ripping Out

I'VE BEGUN EXCAVATION of CONTENT's deck, and the operation reminds me that tearing into old timbers of a wooden boat is, like any archaeological dig, a good way to discover and recall the past. And excavation is what one does. There's no nice, gentlemanly way to go about removing, say, CONTENT's foredeck winch. It's bolted to a this, which is bolted to a that, which is in turn lagged to what might as well be the center of the earth as far as the possibility of getting at the fastenings is concerned. So one excavates. Or rather—wrecking bar, tire iron, pipe wrench, and sledgehammer in hand—one attacks. This phase of the work has very little to do with boat carpentry. It has a lot to do with coal mining.

Not only do nuts not turn off bolts and screws not turn (no matter what one calls them), but even when they are sawn through, heads ground off, shanks chewed through with one's teeth, the parts they fasten refuse to budge. There's an old New England expression to the effect that some boats are held together only through habit. Well, now I know it's no joke.

I know I finally got out all of CONTENT's foredeck winch fastenings after a morning of blaspheming, and gave the winch a triumphant kick, expecting at least to *wiggle* the sonofabitch. It was like kicking St. Paul's Cathedral. I still don't know how I did get the winch out. All I can remember is grabbing my three-foot pipe wrench, and then everything going black.

As I hack, rip, and blast, I unearth little reminders of the past, the days when Nancy and I were discussing the boat with its previous owner. As I pry off the covering board, sure enough, I see for the first time the earthly remains of the ancient iron drifts that once were driven down through the sheerstrake, and I can recall discussing the construction details of the boat with the previous owner. He had been telling me about those very drifts as we sat in the main cabin on a summer day in the Annapolis yacht harbor. We had been going on and on about it, and I suppose my good seawife had begun to feel left out.

I think there's a built-in male chauvinism in any conversation between two male sailors concerning construction details of wooden boats. Somehow, it's OK in this enlightened age for women to win races, skipper charter boats, even take a noon latitude sight, but there's something weird, strange, abnormal, about a woman saying words like "sheerstrake," "rabbet," or "keelson." I know that's sexist, illogical, even dumb, but whaddya gonna do—so sue me.

So, there we were, carrying on as if Nancy weren't even there. The previous owner had worked his way down from the bulwarks to the keel and was happily proclaiming the high quality of her backbone fastenings, Monel and bronze. My wife, quick as a flash, saw her chance to blow the male chauvinist conversation out of the water. "All bronze?" she said. "What about the drift bolts?" It worked like a dose of salts.

"Huh?" the owner said, mastering his awkwardness brilliantly.

"The drift bolts," my wife said. "The drift bolts in the deadwood."

"Gee," he said, "I dunno . . . never thought about it." I thought that following up "drift bolts" with "deadwood" was a masterful stroke. It done the old chap in! From then on, my wife was included in the conversation. As to the deadwood drift bolts, the question remains a mystery. My woodworker's cynicism tells me they're probably composed of three ship augers for each drift, and I suppose the augers are steel.

The various fastenings that I unearth keep reminding me of other events now long passed. As I expose deckbeams, I ruefully remember how the surveyor had told me that he suspected that some of them "weren't right." Well, if they weren't right 10 years ago, I can tell you now that they haven't gotten any better. So far, I've exposed five beams, and the score is zero for five. Gee, they look OK from the outside.

The frames look OK, though, and the sheer clamp is good, so we expect to heal the old girl's age problems in due course. I plan to put on a deck composed of two layers of ½-inch plywood covered with glass.

Now, let those who even now are howling in indignation at the sacrilege of doing away with her planked decks, think on the following. I've heard it all, Mac; hell, I carried on in a similar vein myself . . . once. Let those purists awaken at 3 a.m. with deck juice in their navels before they condemn me.

The man who suggested the plywood-and-glass solution was a local boat carpenter, who listened patiently to my lecture about purity and tradition and then blew my whole oration sky high with three simple but irrefutable words. These words were, "It won't leak." Hours later, I awakened from a troubled sleep as the insight really sank deep into my psyche. I had been made privy to a cosmic truth: "It won't leak."

And I also don't want to hear about other solutions to the leaking deck problem. Things that work on other boats often don't work on CONTENT. Trouble in one area has a way of turning out to be caused by trouble in some other area, sometimes quite remote. As a matter of fact, I just realized why we've had so much trouble with leaking decks all these years. It must be the drift bolts in the deadwood. Probably pure Swedish black iron, notorious causers of leaky decks.

CHAPTER 32

Purists' Revenge

NOW THAT I'VE begun major repairs on CONTENT, people around the boatyard have become much friendlier. They smile and greet me in the morning, even ask how things are going. I don't like it one bit. Just what the hell are they up to? I had thought that once word got around that I was ripping off the 70-year-old kauri pine deck and replacing it with plywood, purists would descend on me from their secret training bases in Mystic, Kennebunk, and Nantucket to take some sort of unspeakable revenge—perhaps force me to go to the next Miami boat show.

I had a friend who once sailed a Friendship sloop that had a Bermuda-rigged mainsail—you know, a sail with only three corners—and people used to threaten him, hurl insults and even beer cans and other solid objects at him. I thought the same sort of thing would happen to me.

However, no one has yelled at me or thrown anything at me. In fact, some of the folks around here have stopped by while I have been at work in order to offer helpful comments and advice. Aha! Maybe that's the explanation for all this friendliness. I'm the victim of a clever conspiracy. They've decided that I'm to be punished by good advice.

I've noticed, for instance, that the advice often comes a day or two too late for me to take advantage of it, unless I were to rip up a lot of work already completed. I've just finished screwing down a sheet of plywood to deckbeams after a week of restoring and replacing those beams, say, and someone will drop an offhand remark like, "If you presoak that plywood in polyhydroglop, it will never rot."

Note the implication that if I do *not* do so, my plywood *will* rot. Of course, now that the plywood is already in place I would have to take it up again or immerse the entire boat in the miracle glop. Of course, I can't afford to immerse the entire boat, and as for undoing what I've already done, even to make things better, I'd rather move to Arizona. So I suppose that for the rest of my days I shall entertain a nagging suspicion that my lovely plywood deck will begin to rot, all for want of timely application of polywhatever.

I can see it now. There's a meeting of purists every other Tuesday. "Has Kasanof finished with his plywood?" they ask. "Good, then it's time to tell him about polyhydroglop; the poor slob will worry about it for years."

Thus do they avenge themselves. And I'm the perfect target for such polysyllabic mind games. I've long since thrown up my hands in despair over the ever-expanding number of synthetic products that are supposed to make life easier for the sailor. Even the world of wooden boats has become infected by the plethora of evil-smelling swill that is supposed to stick wood together, seal it, preserve it, color it, and in general make it peachy keen.

I'm intimidated by it all, but at the same time I have doubts— just as I wonder about the proliferating number of diets. If just one of them really worked, why would we need all the others? Just the other day, someone suggested that I treat my wood with polyester resin and something else—God knows what. Even I know that polyester is a breed of sheep from which we get the polyester wool out of which we weave polyester clothing. So now they've figured out a way to take a traditional natural product and change its form to yet another wood additive. Some may call that progress, but I kind of have a hankering for God's own traditional polyester.

There may even be a supernatural element to my punishment for going modern with CONTENT's decks. My power tools have started to remonstrate with me. The first time I had to make repeated passes through my bandsaw with the plywood, the saw said—with a sad, descending wail—"Why, why, why?" I was so unnerved that I decided to complete the work with a handsaw. That's a lot more work, but I thought I wouldn't have to put up with a lot of philosophical questioning.

Now, hand tools and especially saws have been talking to me for years. Crosscut saws usually say, "Neoprene, neoprene, neoprene" as I saw, but this time my crosscut suddenly began to say, "Weird a-fiend, weird a-fiend, weird a-fiend," as if slandering me with a phony Italian accent. Only a supreme act of will on my part forced it back to good old "neoprene." It's getting so that I'm afraid to turn on any of my power tools. The electric plane has only to be turned on to scream, "Jeez!" at me.

I don't know how my enemies have enlisted the dark powers in order to punish me for my plywood deck, but I'm serving notice that I'm on to them. No more mister nice guy. The next time someone around here tries to be friendly with that, "Hi, Dave, how's it going?" crapola, I'm just going to look right through him and not say anything. If he wants conversation, he can talk to my router.

CHAPTER 33

Navel Preparedness

ICAN'T BELIEVE I am sitting here in the main cabin, doing what I am doing—hoping and waiting for the arrival of my worst enemy, the rain. "Gracious sakes!" you may well exclaim, "why are you doing that, you odd chap?" Well, on this very day I have extended my new plywood deck to the 'midship beam, and I want to see how it feels to not get dripped on when it rains. You know—just the way regular folks feel on *their* boats when it rains.

I know they remain on their boats during rain squalls because I never meet them up at the 7-Eleven store, where I hide out reading the *Journal of the American Neurologic Society* whenever it rains. If they're not at the 7-Eleven, the Palais de Versailles of the social whirl here along the New River, where else are they but on their boats? Surely they're not watching the colorful peasant folk downtown at the village fountain—you know the one, in front of the banking complex, where the peasants come in their native garb, sunglasses and sharkskin suits, to launder their money—no, no. I'm tired of skulking about the 7-Eleven while everyone who is anyone is laughing at the rain, snug and dry on boats whose decks don't leak.

That is why I am waiting for my enemy of old. When the rain comes, I shall join the honorable company of boat people with dry navels. I want to know the joy of looking up at a sky during a rain squall and not getting precipitated on in the eye.

Naturally the rain, because I desire it, seems to have held off for the past several days, despite this being the beginning of the rainy season. It's the well-known principle by which taking an umbrella ensures dry weather. I know the rain will come soon, though, not because of the season but because of something more sinister.

Although I have taken infinite pains with my new deck, glued and screwed to a fare-thee-well, I know the nature of the universe, especially as it applies to water. The universe, as I have pointed out in previous lectures, is neither good nor bad; it is something much worse. The universe is a pain in the ass. Water that will not run through a two-inch limber hole blocked by a marmoset's nasal hair, will rush in a torrent through a microscopic flaw in a fiber of deck plank, provided that the leak is directly over my soup.

When it rains, and I believe I can see the storm clouds gathering in the west, I know that my problems won't be over—not completely. Oh yes, they'll be much less severe. Two layers of ½-inch plywood glued and screwed together with no overlapping seams have got to take care of most of the problem, but there remains the possibility of an inexplicable leak.

I am prepared for the seam between the skylight and the deck to leak. I am prepared for the skylight itself to leak (after all, that's what skylights are for, isn't it?). What I am not prepared for, yet half expectant of, is an inexplicable leak, a leak that causes one to cry out with the sailor's ancient lament, "Where in hell is it getting in?"

In my mind's eye I can see it—a hanging droplet of water smack in the middle of an expanse of dry overhead, far from any seam, with no telltale streak of water leading to its origin. I wipe it away, but slowly it grows again. It is an incubus, an evil djinn, come to torment me in my dotage. It is an inexplicable leak.

I do not know what I shall do if such an event does occur, but moving to Denver is a viable option. I feel that after 10 years of running around the boat with a flashlight marking leaks with a pencil, pouring hundreds of dollars into strip-planked deck seams to no significant avail, taping up pieces of plastic bag to save vital equipment such as the TV, I deserve a leak-free old age.

"I deserve?" I can hear the gods chuckle at the phrase. Here comes the squall. Neither I—nor the rabbit in the hawk's talons, nor the sailor looking for the outer range flasher on a thick night—*deserve* anything. Ya takes what's dished out, Mac. I know all that. But, dammit—I deserve a dry deck.

Oh, boy, here comes the rain. The first big drops of a tropical downpour splatter on the skylight. So far, so good—it's not soaking through the glass. Oops! There's one, coming through right there at the corner of the skylight, probably through the dovetail joint; OK, I can fix that. And there—that one's probably getting in through the empty screw hole at the top of the skylight. I'll run a screw in there and fill it with compound. What, you say? Look over there, where any leak would be inexplicable? Not until I get confirmation of my Denver flight reservation.

CHAPTER 34

The Imperfect Tool for Every Job

IN MY NEVER-ENDING quest for truth and justice, I have frequently encountered myths and falsehoods foisted on an unsuspecting public by the massed powers of darkness. On such occasions I have never hesitated to set things right, heedless of my own welfare. Once again, dear comrades, I couch my lance in a just cause.

I have encountered a terrible and sinful lie about the proper use of tools, and, to compound the crime, the lie is told to our young people (our young people!) in a book that purports to instruct them in basic shop techniques. The naive youngster is, first off, told that the screwdriver is for driving or removing screws. The author even has the gall to say, "Never pound on the screwdriver handle with a hammer. Remember, the screwdriver is not a chisel."

The hell it ain't. Often, the screwdriver is the best damn chisel or any other tool in the toolbox. How else are you going to get the dried paint out of the screw slot or force the corner of the blade into the center of a Phillips-head screw, other than by pounding on the screwdriver? Grudgingly, I admit that a hammer is not always the best pounder. If the job is a big one and you're *really* ticked off, a pipe wrench or wrecking bar is nice. A screwdriver works better than any chisel for excavation work and for opening paint cans. A screwdriver not a chisel? Tosh—a screwdriver is virtually anything you want it to be. I have used mine for (in addition to chisel and can-opener) a nail set, center-punch, star drill, wood bit, nut splitter, and hot-wire finder (the latter not always intentionally).

As for using a screwdriver for backing screws out—that claim leaves me speechless. In the real world of wooden boats, the *last* tool I reach for in such a case is the screwdriver, unless of course, I intend to put it to its proper use—as a chisel; that is, to pound hell on its handle in order to excavate enough wood to enable the Vise Grips to get a bite. Anyone with experience working on old wooden boats (I confine my remarks to old wooden boats because there is no such a thing as a new wooden boat) knows that a screwdriver can't be used as a screwdriver on old screws, because (a) the slot cannot be found;

(b) even if it could, it would be of the type opposite to the type of screwdriver that you can find; and (c) the wood around the screw head has mysteriously grown inward so that the hole is smaller than the screw that made it.

As if not satisfied merely by words to infect our young people with his never-never-land mystique concerning the screwdriver, this miscreant supplies an illustration that makes matters even worse. The illustration shows a handsome smiling man, dressed in *clean clothes*, kneeling comfortably, while turning in a screw with apparent ease. Again, the author seems to live on some ideal plane. Everyone knows that the damn screw won't go, not in the real world where the rest of us live, not driven by some Mr. Cleanclothes, smiling and comfortable.

The accompanying text advises the reader to "Let the tool do the work; don't strain or force it." Brothers and sisters, how in the pluperfect hell are you going to get the bloody screw either in or out unless you bust a living gut?

That text should have read, "The screw is your enemy. You hate it. It must die. Place the screwdriver in the slot and pound the bejeezus out of the screw in order to drive out residual gunk from the slot, to separate the screw threads from the wood fibers, and to punish the screw. Now place the handle of the screwdriver in the pit of your stomach. Engage the square part of the screwdriver shaft with Vise Grips. (If your screwdriver has a round shaft, give it to someone you don't like.) Lunge against the screwdriver with all your weight while simultaneously turning the screwdriver via the Vise Grips and bellowing insults against the screw and the screw's mother. This will round off the slot edges or break the screw shaft. See next chapter on Extreme Measures."

That's the way it is down here in the real world, where nothing fits, nothing is straight or parallel, and nothing ever quite works the way it says in the owner's manual. Believing in smiling men in clean clothing, comfortably driving in screws, soon leads to believing that crooks get caught, that it's not winning that matters but how you play the game, that truth will always out. In short, one kind of tooth fairy begets another.

It's especially important for those of the wooden boat tribe to keep a keen eye on the hard, practical realities. After all, isn't that why we sail old gaffers with tanbark sails, deadeyes, baggywrinkles, squaresails, and gunports?

CHAPTER 35

The Old Second Sea Dog Trick

E VERY DAIRY FARMER knows that if you have a lazy cow dog, all you have to do is get a second dog, a good one, and the first dog will work his butt off not to be outdone. I spent a good part of my youth on a small dairy farm and learned this trick before I'd reached my teens, but only recently have I learned that it works with hand tools as well.

I should have realized it sooner, because, as readers of this column know, I was the first researcher to publish findings indicating that there are no such things as inanimate objects; that all objects—at least on boats—are not only self-conscious beings but malevolent beings. Now, I can report that at least one species of object, the brace-and-bit, is not only self-conscious and malevolent but smart—at least as smart as a cow dog.

The ratchet on my 20-year-old brace had not worked properly in 19 years and 11 months, so I promptly got a new one at a local flea market. I knew it was a good one because I shelled out four dollars—cash—for it. When I got back to the boat, I threw it into the tool bin and picked up my old brace before tossing it into the dumpster. As I prepared to heave it, there came the clickety-click of a perfectly healthy ratchet, a sound I had not heard for 19 years and 11 months.

Until that moment, that god-forsaken thing had been frozen solid. It had resisted all assaults by modern technology, including particle-beam accelerators, a high-intensity laser, even Liquid Wrench and the most creative blast of obscenities ever heard this side of the Tom Bigby River. Yet, 10 seconds after seeing that new brace, the old one began to straighten up and fly right, and it has held to the path of righteousness ever since. Smart? Don't talk to me about your cow dogs, brother; I can tell you about smart.

Take fiberglass, for instance. I've been putting this god-awful stuff on CONTENT's new decks, and it's my first experience with what L. Francis Herreshoff aptly called "congealed snot." People warned me that it is tricky material to work with, but nobody warned me about how *smart* it is. At least, it's a lot smarter than I am.

The cloth is the really smart stuff. It knows just how to distort so that when you think you're cutting it straight across, you find out that you've cut it diagonally, and wiggly as well. It also likes to grab you and not let go. It sends out fine tendrils that invisibly engage your clothing so that when you stand up after carefully positioning the cloth, it seems to rise magically from its appointed position to follow and mock you.

It does no good to get mad in this situation, because the cloth can fight back. If you really get hysterical with rage, you can beat the hell out of your brace-and-bit and it won't fight back; but fiberglass cloth is a close relative of the jellyfish known as the Portuguese man-of-war, and if you get physically abusive with it, you will soon become better acquainted with recent advances in dermatologic therapy.

Like many intelligent beings, fiberglass cloth is quick to recognize the novice. In fact, I seem to recall something like a smirk on the surface of the first roll of cloth that I bought. Perhaps I should not have allowed it to overhear as I asked the man which was the glass and which was the resin. On the other hand, even if it had not overheard, my inexperience probably would have been immediately apparent during the first few moments of attempting to work with the material, in much the same way that a saddle horse recognizes an inexperienced rider right away—although I don't for a moment wish to imply, however obliquely, that horses are as smart as fiberglass.

It wouldn't have taken much smarts, though, to identify me as a novice fiberglasser as I tried to fight off strips of cloth that didn't want to be let go of or as I tried to get bubbles out of cloth that refused to lie flat despite oceans of resin and the frantic ministrations of a tool that the man in the store called a "bubble chaser." In my hands it became a bubble multiplier. The answer I found was to allow the bubbles to set, then grind them off and apply more resin. I've tried everything else—threats, pleading, arguments— but all to no avail. Surely the ultimate solution is for me to get smarter than the fiberglass, but who can wait that long?

CHAPTER 36

Tumblehome Sweet Home

MAYBE I WILL have to stop making fun of "character boats." That's a shame, because it's fun to make fun of boats with false clipper bows, gun ports, and baggywrinkle all over the place. I used to have a condescending attitude toward the Bristol Channel cutter, which CONTENT somewhat resembles, because the Bristol cutter has a more "yachty" look. CONTENT, by contrast, is about as yachty as a clam dredger. "Yes," I would say, "very lovely, and that pretty tumblehome aft improves the look of the transom and allows the 12-pounder cannon to lodge closer to the centerline." Thus, with a smirk, could I badmouth a fine boat. I once considered offering a prize for anyone who could come up with a good reason for tumblehome other than "style"; if I had, I think my money would still be safe. Tumblehome probably began with a loftsman who was running out of room on the lofting floor or who couldn't find the ship curve he needed.

But all that smart-mouthing is a thing of the past. I have just discovered that CONTENT was originally constructed with slight tumblehome starting about 18 inches forward of her transom. So I am now desperately seeking some plausible-sounding rationale for CONTENT's new-found "yachtiness." It doesn't have to *be* plausible; it just has to *sound* plausible. By definition, if CONTENT has it, it's gotta be practical and earthy. I'm open to suggestion but please spare me all that crap about Thames measurement, gun emplacement, and fair leading of standing rigging. I gotta have something that applies to modern sailing vessels during the early part of the 20th century. You know, like . . . "tumblehome had a renaissance early in this century because of the Teapot Dome scandal." You take it from there.

So that's my problem—how to explain CONTENT's tumblehome after going on record as a scoffer. But, you ask, aren't you overlooking another problem? I was about to get to that. The other problem goes, "How can anyone be such a lard-head that he can live aboard a boat for 12 years and not realize what the hull looks like?"

Simple. CONTENT's tumblehome is a *secret* tumblehome. Anyone with an old wooden boat knows that just because the frames do one

100

thing, it doesn't mean the planking has to slavishly do the same thing. No, no, you naive old chap. CONTENT's last two frames tumble home, but her planking goes on unperturbed, to land gracefully on a transom that has been cut to where the planks end, not to where the transom frame is or where the loftsman made his silly tick marks (assuming that CONTENT was lofted, a proposition that grows more dubious as I observe her in ever greater detail).

I noticed the occult tumblehome only when I had ripped up the aftermost part of her deck, preparatory to installing new deckbeams and a new deck. There, bathed in tropical sunlight, lay the evidence that had been hidden either from the time of CONTENT's building or the time, some 40 years ago, when her new transom and sternpost had been put in. (She was once clobbered by a gravel barge.) The planking had simply been allowed to spring away from the frames, eliminating the yachty transom shape.

Now comes the moment of truth. After years of smirking at such cute "character boat" baubles as tumblehome, what should I do about CONTENT's newly discovered secret? It would be easy just to ignore it, redeck her, and not say anything. Well, I just can't do it. Partly, it would bother me to think of those planks three or four inches away from the frames, but that's not the real reason that I shall restore the original tumblehome. The real reason is that when I first noticed the original shape of the transom—I admit it—I liked it.

It was like discovering a secret compartment in a desk one has owned for years—but there was an added element. This was not just tumblehome—an easy mark for satire. This was CONTENT's tumblehome, tumblehome not to be judged by the petty standards of other boats.

So I shall do two things. I shall continue to smirk at so-called "character boats" with their old-timey cuteness, but I shall bring those planks in to the after frames and recut the transom accordingly. How will I be able to deride the tumblehome of other boats when I have painstakingly restored CONTENT's own? I don't know yet, but I'll find a way. As mentioned, explanations of this sort have to sound plausible, down-to-earth, and practical. I kind of like the idea of linking her tumblehome to the Teapot Dome scandal, but I'm afraid someone might ask me what that is.

CHAPTER 37

Supernatural Stresses

SOME PEOPLE are just born worriers, and I suppose I must be one of them. I thought that once I got old CONTENT hauled out of the water, my life would change, that joy and happiness would be mine. I would look forward to the repair phase with optimism and would be able to stop worrying about what might be going on unseen below the waterline. I would also be able to stop worrying about sinking during the night.

Well, CONTENT is now hauled out, and I'm here to tell you, folks, that nothing ever changes. I'm looking forward to the repair phase with fear and dread, and I still haven't the foggiest about what might be going on unseen below the waterline—except that I'm pretty sure it ain't good. The fact that I can walk around the hull and examine every part close up hasn't helped; it has only brought the mystery into clearer focus. I mean, for instance, that the questionable area in the stem doesn't just go from here to there; it goes all the way from *here* to way over *there*. But I still don't know what's really wrong.

Sure, sure, I should stop worrying about it and begin the excavation, but I need a little time to catch my breath first. After all, one of the worst mistakes a wooden boat owner can make is to be prematurely accurate in assessing the enormity of the task before him. Hell, if most of us had had any brains in the beginning we'd still be living ashore, probably in Sandusky, Ohio. So, I really don't want to know too much too soon. Worry might not be very pleasant, but it could be a damn sight better than really knowing what the problems are. I am reminded of an old saying, "If you can keep calm when those about you have given way to despair, you probably don't understand the problem."

If being hauled out has, admittedly, eased a worry here and there (after all, the old girl probably won't sink . . . I guess), it has introduced new ones, in addition to the traditional nautical ones. Now, I worry about the boat falling over on its side. I worry about raccoons running down my bowsprit from where it juts into the treetops across the canal. I worry about falling off the ladder. In fact, what if someone made off with the ladder while I was away? How would I get back aboard? Do I want to get back aboard? The mind boggles.

Another source of worry is quite sinister, even chilling. Every folk tradition has spooky tales about corpses that refuse to stay buried. I shudder to report that the phenomenon is not an old wives' tale nor limited to the departed. My telephone cable has been exhibiting this eerie proclivity. Let me explain.

CONTENT has been moved to a part of the yard that makes it necessary for the traveling crane to pass between CONTENT and our telephone jack. Cars and pedestrians must also pass this way, so things like utility cords must be buried, and it is up to the boat owner to do that. Now, I never claimed to be an expert telephone-cord burier, but I thought I had done a fair-to-middlin' job of it and, for several days, like any ghost-story character of the deceased persuasion, the damn thing stayed buried.

Then, one dark and stormy night, I was awakened from a restless slumber by my pet raven crying, "Dig it deeper, dig it deeper." Sure enough, there in the ghastly moonlight lay several feet of cord that had apparently struggled upward to rejoin the world of humans, impelled by who knows what unspeakable forces. The next morning I buried it again, adding a sprinkling of wolfsbane and garlic for good measure.

Anyone who has ever read a book or been to the movies knows the rest. I would bury it here, and it would pop up somewhere else. It would stay buried for a day or two, I would start to relax, and someone would say, "Kasanof, you better bury that cable before someone trips over it."

Finally, one day, when I was over in the shop area for another jar of wolfsbane and garlic, one of the yard employees suggested that I use the pickaxe kept in the shop for such purposes. I suppose he had taken pity on me after watching me, armed only with a wrecking bar and a rich vocabulary, struggle with Florida limestone. I thanked him and made a "proper job" of burying the restless cord quite a bit deeper. That was several days ago, and there have been no nocturnal stirrings as yet. It's too soon, though, to write, "In Pace Requiescat."

Unfortunately, I can't hope for the winter hardness of the ground to keep the thing buried, because the ground doesn't get hard here in Paradise. But temperatures get low enough to make it pretty cold aboard a boat that no longer has the warming effect of surrounding water. In addition, the boat has dried out to the extent that her planks have shrunk and the wind whistles through the open seams like a prairie gale through a squatter's cabin.

Add that to the list of worries attendant on being hauled out: Will it get much colder? What happened to our little electric heater? If CONTENT's timbers shrink even more, will she fall apart one icy morning with a great clatter? I recall that a wise old sailor once told me that the stresses on a wooden boat under sail are nowhere near as great as the stresses she must undergo when hauled out, and that she must withstand those stresses just when her structural integrity is at its lowest ebb, due to shrinkage of her members away from their fastenings.

He was right, but he didn't realize the other half of that essential truth. The stresses on the skipper are just as great, and he has to deal with the supernatural.

CHAPTER 38

As Time Goes By

WHEN I'M TEMPTED to look back on all the years CONTENT's had possession of me, instead of feeling satisfied with what's been accomplished, I am sobered by the realization that during those same years it has taken me to get where I am with her, entire municipal transport systems have been created, hydroelectric plants have been completed, whole political careers have gone their progress from election to indictment, trial, and conviction. We've come a long way, but it has taken some time. A lot of water has run under the keel or, more accurately, dripped through the deck seams since I first decided to renew CONTENT's tired old bones.

Many years ago, I believed that there was a simple solution to her problems, the dour warnings of experienced boatwrights notwithstanding. New materials, I thought, must surely have rendered their "rip it out and do it over" advice obsolete. As soon as I began to encounter 14 different types of old glop from previous owners' attempts to do things the easy way, I should have realized that that counsel had been right. I should have realized that if any of this stuff had worked, there would have been no need for 14 varieties.

I look back on this and wonder how we lived through it all. We kept dry by skillful placing of pots and pans and adept manipulation of plastic garbage bags. The trick was to cut a plastic bag on two sides so that it could be transformed into a single flat sheet. Then we would tape the plastic sheet to the deckbeams so that it would catch the drips. As the drips accumulated at the low point, a plastic boil would form. We would lance this boil and place a pot under the discharge. You won't find yachtsy little tricks like that in Hervey Garrett Smith.

Now, many years later, CONTENT boasts a new fiberglass and plywood deck (Oh, be quiet!), and we live in dry comfort no matter how hard it rains. That is because we now live in a trailer, but I do not want to bore you with details. We've moved ashore because I am now sistering frames, have gutted the inside of the boat, and not even the hardy Kasanofs can live aboard under those conditions. I know that our decks are now tight because of our cat. Only our cat continues to live aboard, and on my daily visits to the boat, I always feel the cat. The cat has always been dry, so I infer tight decks.

When I look at CONTENT today, it pains me to recall that a few years ago we could actually sail her. Her new deck is void of cleats, pinrails, mainsheet traveler, etc., but piled high with junk from below. Below, she looks even worse, with her cabin sole ripped up and rusted-out water tanks, tools, and lumber sitting where people used to be. She looks like dozens of boats that I have been aboard over the years and thought of the owner, "What that poor dumb bastard has in store for him!" I am nevertheless sustained by faith (i.e., belief without basis in reason or facts) that CONTENT must in the nature of things look worse before she looks better, like someone with an upper respiratory infection. Currently, she is in a stage of recovery that in a human would correspond to mucus and horrible chest noises. In fact, her bilge pump, when it sucks air, sounds like . . . well, you get the picture.

Of course, one cannot contemplate the past without thinking about the future. When I do this, a simple calculation comes to mind with depressing plausibility. If it has taken me 10 years to do about one-quarter of the job, it should take me another 30 to complete it. That is, when I am ready to go cruising, I shall be as old as Mozart was when he had been dead half a century.

Thank goodness, there are several ways out of this iron logic. One way is to ignore logic; an ability that every wooden boat owner who would preserve his sanity would do well to cultivate. Another is to assume that the previous rate of progress will accelerate. In my case, the second solution may not be entirely bogus. After all, for the first few years of our tenure, I was busy five days a week pretending that I was a regular mainstream guy. I had a suit and a briefcase and I flew in airplanes and wrote memos and all that stuff. Now that I am no longer respectable, I think the boat work will go much faster.

Check with me in about 30 years. If I haven't gone to join Mozart, I hope to be full of blue-water cruising stories by then. Either that, or I'll still be wondering about how to fit a new stem. If that's the case, I'll probably be happily divorced from reality. Instead of checking with me, better go right to the nurses' station.

CHAPTER 39

Just Measure and Cut

TO FURTHER MY campaign to erode standards of boat carpentry, I offer the following revision to the well-known maxim, "Measure twice; cut once": "Measure only once, or you may not have the nerve to cut at all."

This new maxim is especially suited to the wooden boat carpenter. The trouble with the old maxim, I have found, is that if you measure twice, the second measurement is either different (as on CONTENT) or it is the same (as in books). If it is different, you have to measure again and again, not just again, because the third measurement only makes it "two out of three," thus leaving the issue still in doubt—unless, of course, the third measurement is different from either the first or second (as on CONTENT). If the second measurement is the same, it might be due to duplicating the same error (as on CONTENT), so you had better measure a third time, just to make sure. Of course, if you *do* measure a third time and it confirms either the first or second measurement, that's still only two out of three, and we've already covered that. Finally, if the third measurement agrees with the first two, it is either correct or due to a systematic error in the method of measurement. Since no amount of subsequent measurement can ever resolve the issue (see "Critique of Empirical Method: Philosophy 201" in the undergraduate catalog), one is best advised to just measure and cut.

What's that? Suppose the piece doesn't fit? Big deal; why do you suppose God gave us shims and filler glop?

I discovered this great principle while getting out floor timbers for CONTENT. I started by making careful measurements but soon ran into the problems I've been explaining. If you do something often enough, you'll do it wrong sooner or later . . . and sooner if you're upside down with your head in the bilge, trying to manipulate a steel tape and a pencil while sweat runs into your eyes.

All of which reminds me of a closely related problem. A major source of error, even in the unlikely event that you've measured correctly, lies in how you mark your measurement with the pencil and where you actually cut in relation to the pencil mark. Do you leave the line, cut right down the line, or "scant" the measurement by cutting inside the line? Don't you dare tell me that the question is easily resolved by looking at each situation intelligently. Do you suppose that if I had any intelligence in excess of my shoe size I would be hanging upside down with my head in the bilge of a 75-year-old wooden boat, sweat running into my eyes, wrestling with a steel tape and pencil (Eberhart-Faber No. 2)?

Even if I could make the right decision where to cut, I am quite capable of (a) forgetting what I decided before I can get to the bandsaw, or (b) forgetting which side of the line is the work side and which is scrap. The latter error usually occurs with rectangular pieces where the scrap and work sides are of similar lengths. In fact, here's a tip for beginners and veterans alike: If the piece you cut doesn't fit, try the piece that is left over. What the hell, sometimes you get lucky.

This business of only cutting once is largely a matter of ego, anyway. It has little to do with quality. If the truth were told, a determined amateur can produce good work by the "cut and try" method. In fact, the amateur can often turn out work superior to that of the professional by this time-honored procedure. He may waste some time and lumber, but the end result will be better. As a matter of fact, he may not even waste as much time as one might suppose. It can take as much time to "get it right the first time" as to "cut and try" until it almost fits. Admittedly, there's a certain intellectual satisfaction in cutting a complex shape and having it fit the first time, but who cares, as long as you end up with a good job?

I learned everything I probably don't know from an old boat carpenter whose challenge to me was, "Kid, when you can make a perfect cube with hand tools, you'll be a master carpenter." Of course, I immediately began to try to make one. I soon found out that a cube has six sides that are interrelated in a most annoying manner. Louse up one side and you louse up at least three and possibly four of the remainder. (Only the opposite side is immune.) I soon realized that I would not live long enough to succeed, so I did the next best thing; I gave up.

So, Van, if you ever read this in the great spar shed in the sky, the world will have to manage without perfect cubes, at least of my manufacture, and my floor timbers will do the job and don't look too bad. That is, they won't after I get enough red lead on them to cover where I slipped in the shims. By the way, the shims fit on the first try . . . after I trimmed off the excess and filled the voids with glop.

CHAPTER 40

Confessions of a House Carpenter

THE LOVE OF wooden boats and traditional methods of maintenance has provided a pleasing vantage point from which I have been able to observe, over the years, my own moral decay. Really, now, to fully enjoy one's moral decay one must have concrete evidence of it, not just vague feelings. CONTENT has amply provided this evidence.

Years ago, the first great falling from a state of purity came with the decision to replace her strip-planked decks (kauri pine, yet) with plywood (gasp) and fiberglass (double gasp). I decided that it was better to be a dry compromiser than a wet purist.

Unfortunately, I had overlooked the possibility of becoming a wet compromiser. This was the result of my having to leave the job uncompleted for many years and having done a less-than-adequate job on the completed part (but we won't go into that, will we?).

Now that I believe I know how to do the job right, I find that I have taken another step down the road to moral turpitude. I have chosen to drill my screw holes with tapered bits. Maybe I should explain myself.

Many years ago, when I was very young and the Indian subcontinent had not yet collided with the Asian mainland, my boat carpentry guru was a man named Pruitt. (God, I hope he doesn't read this!) Van Pruitt believed that a sloppy job was not just a sloppy job; it was an offense in the eyes of God, an unspeakable anathema. Worse, it was bad carpentry. If pressed too hard about the reason for doing something in a certain way, he would declaim, "Because master carpenter Pruitt says that that is the way to do it!"

One day, Pruitt saw me fitting a tapered bit into my drill.

"What in the bloody hell is that?" he inquired pleasantly.

"A tapered bit."

"Except for right at the point, does the thread of your screw taper?"

"No, sir."

"Does the shank of the screw taper?"

"No, sir."

109

"Then why in the bloody hell are you drilling a hole whose profile nowhere matches the profile of your screw?"

Then he added the epithet I was to hear many times, a term of extreme abuse: "House carpenter."

Ever since, I have felt morally constrained to drill two holes for each screw, sometimes three when counterbores were required, if I couldn't find a combination bit that fit the job. I often used two drills or changed bits for every damn hole.

But now I have fallen again. As I put my new tapered bit into the chuck, I said, "I know, Mr. Pruitt, but I have hundreds of holes to drill." Then I drilled into two pieces of scrap to check that I had the right bit, and turned in the screw with another drill fitted with a screwdriver bit. The screw socked up tighter than Yancey's goat, and I knew I was hooked for life. Ah! All those wasted years righteously performing all those extra drilling operations! Too soon old; too late smart.

Alas, I had just begun my slide to perdition. I had to replace a rotten "stealer" plank near the stern. My new ¾ mahogany plank had to take a 30-degree twist in its four-foot length, and I had never done this type of job before. However, I had read a lot about it and was confident that my "book larnin'" would enable me to do a nice job.

Indeed, the pattern I made did fit perfectly, and the plank, of course, fit the pattern. Things didn't begin to fall apart until I began to tighten the bolts (I couldn't trust screws to hold that twist in). A corner of the narrow end of the plank began to gouge into the frame instead of twisting, and the entire plank began to migrate upward with every turn of the nut, so that in the end the upper seam was too tight, and had to be opened up with a sabersaw, while the bottom seam was too broad.

A voice from the past said, "Do it again, house carpenter, and this time, try drilling your holes at right angles to the face of the work." Did I heed the voice? Hell, no. In fact, my main concern was to get the job caulked, seamed, and painted before a real boat carpenter saw it. I rushed to hide my shame behind a facade of glop.

What, after all, is one to expect from someone so far sunk in depravity that he has already used tapered bits? I was reminded of an 18th-century wit who said that a man, once stooped to commit murder, would soon progress to lying, procrastination, and, finally, rudeness.

And so, down the slippery slope I slid, caulking away like mad with an iron that didn't really fit (a step up from my usual screwdriver) and a large ball-peen hammer. I threw seam compound and paint over the whole mess just in the nick of time before a real boat carpenter walked by. He said, "Good morning," without a trace of a snicker, and I thought I had made it. But life isn't that simple.

The next minute, for the first time in my life, I came face to face with a real professional caulker. I mean, this guy had a leather bag with 50 irons in it, mallets that he had made, and a dropped right shoulder from 60 years of caulking wooden boats. How glad I was that he had not seen what I had just perpetrated on my own seams. He scrutinized my job for a few seconds and then, for some unfathomable reason, began to give me a lecture-demonstration of the right way to caulk a boat.

It was fascinating and I am truly grateful for his efforts, but in my secret heart I know that I shall continue with the screwdriver and hammer, as long as no one is looking, of course. I shall probably need some extra cotton, though, to plug my ears against a certain voice that I know will be saying, "Master carpenter Pruitt says that's not the way to do it . . . house carpenter."

PART FOUR

Meditations
from the Fo'c's'le

CHAPTER 41

True Friend of My Youth

A S I APPROACH a well-earned senility, I have become accustomed to the comfortable notion that even though my backbone is hogged, my planks sprung, and my poor old frame long since sailed out of shape, my knowledge has increased, expanded, deepened; I am, in fact, fast becoming that character out of the Christmas cards and boutique-boat shoppe lampshades—the old shellback himself. However, just a little while ago, I discovered that that idea has got to go to the slag heap along with my reaction time and aerobic capacity. I haven't been getting smarter, I have been getting dumber. I haven't been adding to my store of knowledge of things nautical; I have been shedding facts like galvanized fastenings out of a 40-year-old dragger's garboards.

Nonsense, say you? A lament of the male menopause? Would that it were so! But the proof bubbled to the surface over a discussion of knots and fancy ropework in CONTENT's snug cabin late this past winter. Sailors of traditional bent, not to say warp, are fond of the esoterica of sail, the antique, and the farther removed from practical utility the better. No colleague during one of our late-night impromptu gatherings aboard the old hooker ever initiated a discussion of the latest changes in *Notice to Mariners* that might affect how we get into and out of our harbor. We have had, on the other hand, several vicious belaying pin fights over the naming of the old THOMAS LAWSON's seven masts—and the man who writes in saying they were actually called after the days of the week had better not sign his name.

That is why that recent discussion of knots was so focused on the arcane. That is why we had many words on the Japanese masthead knot, the English diamond knot, and the Carrick bend, but no words on the bowline (although there are four correct ways to tie it) or the rolling hitch (although it's almost always incorrectly illustrated). Now, all through this discussion I could be heard saying, "Oh, yeah—I used to know how to tie that one!" Someone would say something about the Matthew Walker and I would say, once again, "Oh yeah—I used to know how to tie that one!" And it's true, the Diamond, the masthead, the Matthew Walker, several kinds of Carrick bend, all were once in my repertoire. That was when I first became interested in boats, some 30 years ago. Now I suppose I know a dozen or so, and the sheepshank I learned as a cub scout, so I guess that doesn't count—useless damn knot anyway. Oh, I suppose I can still whip up a passable Turk's head but the last time I tied one I bit through my lower lip.

It's a sign of age, you see. I'm no longer interested in the thing just for the perverse pleasure of it. If a knot doesn't do a job I need done fairly often, I chuck it. How prosaic, but there's grey, palsied dotage for you. Strangely, it's different in non-nautical areas. In them, advancing years brings greater interest in the impractical, at least if general cultural interests are a gauge. And yet, what could be more cultural than a Matthew Walker, well tied of course? Cleating a line properly, making a good serviceable splice, that's working on boats—but a Matthew Walker, man, that's culture. So, by rights, I ought to be interested in the Matthew Walker but I'm not; just looking at Figure 4 makes me tired.

Even the ropework that I do know is deteriorating, as modern materials pass me by. For instance, I used to disdain the so-called "sailmaker's whipping" as unnecessary, and indeed it was once just so. "Common whipping" was secure enough—for a time. But along came Nylon and Dacron line, some of it slippery as a Philadelphia lawyer, and lately some of my old whipping has begun to slide off the end of the line. My good seawife is currently trying to teach me a sailmaker's whipping but I haven't gotten it yet. Maybe late one night I'll sneak out on deck and fuse the ends of all my plastic line with a match, or put one of those heat-setting plastic collars around the ends. Then I could do my common whipping over the heat-sealed or be-collared line and . . . ah . . . with my luck I'd probably set fire to some good old manila, true friend of my youth.

CHAPTER 42

Twaddle and Non-Twaddle

THERE ARE TWO kinds of sailorly knowledge: book knowledge and doing knowledge, or more accurately put, twaddle and non-twaddle. Twaddle can be amusing, even useful, but it's a mistake to take it for the genuine article. Most twaddle gets written by sailors who read too much, and believed by sailors like me who in turn write it down or say it to other sailors, who in turn . . . One is soon disenchanted when one actually tries to put some of this bookish lore into practice. That generally occurs at 0400 hours during an onshore gale, or at 90 degrees Fahrenheit with the boat hauled out in a yard that charges by the day.

I don't recall when I first read that cotton should be driven into topside seams until the mallet "rings." I know that I have read many references to the ringing of caulking mallets in "the old days." Twaddle! I had occasion not long ago to caulk a few of old CONTENT's seams, due to a rare navigational indiscretion. The caulking mallet had slots cut in it to mislead the gullible into believing that, properly used, the mallet would ring when striking the making iron. At first it went "tick tick," then changed to "tack tack" as I drove the cotton in, finally evolving into "thwock thwock," at which point I gave up the attempt to make it do anything resembling ringing. Maybe the laws of acoustics have changed and maybe I'm not the most skillful caulker on the coast but, by Godfrey, I can do two things: I can pour water out of my boots, and I can tell "thwock thwock" from "ding dong!" Ding dong is what bells do and thwock thwock is what caulking mallets do and I don't want to hear any more about it!

My bookish knowledge of how to use a serving mallet is almost as old as my caulking expertise. My real-life experience began late last winter when I learned that it isn't like *Chapman's*, or whomever—*almost*—but the differences are enough to drive a poor sailor lad to golf. The difficulty lies in passing the ball of marline around what you're trying to serve, as you rotate the serving mallet around it. Now, you can do this with a second "man" or, in my case, wife, functioning as the "passer," and this works well—one reads. Twaddle! It doesn't work at all, for the passer will soon begin to give the server advice. What's more, if the passer has the effrontery to give *good* advice, the damaging effect on human relationships can be profound.

My attempted solution to this was to stick the ball of marline on the handle of the mallet and try to feed marline from the ball. Damn, hadn't I seen diagrams of that many times in books? Shipmates, those diagrams, I'm here to tell you, were drawn by three-armed servers. If you don't hold the ball with one hand it will fall off the end of the handle when the handle is pointing down. Clever stops on the end of the handle, designed to prevent this, (yeah, yeah—I thought of that, too!) interfere with how the marline comes off the ball. Finally, if you try to hang on to the ball as you rotate the mallet, you either break the marline because of too much tension or release too much tension and ruin what you've done.

My own solution was a clever compromise between holding and not holding the marline ball. I retained it with a rubber band (how unshippy!), which the books don't mention. This caused me to both drop the blasted ball when the band broke and break the marline when I got too much friction around the mallet's head and handle. I must say, though, I did finally finish the job, which was to renew the serving on my two gaff bridles. Application of Stockholm tar over the finished job hid most of my sins and the second bridle went much smoother. Unfortunately, when the mains'l is raised, you can tell from the deck which bridle I did first.

One of the prime, and potentially dangerous bits of twaddle lurking about in books to snag the unwary sailor-scholar, is that business about scandalizing the main of a gaff-rigged boat. I've seen that one with reference to gybing and seen it recommended as a quick way to "reef" in a blow. It's said that the way to gybe is to drop the peak, gybe, then peak up the main after completing the gybe. Sounds great as long as one confines the maneuver to conditions that render it unnecessary. I know that in a blow, if I dropped CONTENT's peak I would instantly turn her main into a loosely billowing nightmare in a sail loft. If I then attempted to gybe that nightmare, I would probably be lucky to get away with just a shredded main. And what do the writers of such advice think happens to a 22-foot gaff in a 30-knot duster when no longer controlled by the tension of the mains'l? I'll tell you what happens. About $2.75 per board foot and a lot of grief is what happens. Not that I ever tried it. I have been forewarned by experience— for once.

I had dropped the peak just a bit to spill some air on a dusty day in Block Island Sound. Block Island Sound, if you've never sailed there, is a body of water in which a hard sneeze will raise a chop that persists for three days—four, if you've been taking snuff. It spilled the wind all right, relieving all stabilizing tension on the gaff, which began flopping about like Hogan's barndoor, as CONTENT, no longer steadied by her sail, tried to roll her stick out. My wife, who had been striving and succeeding in preparing supper up to this point, yelled out the forward hatch, "Less reading and more reefing—quit experimenting!"

Reefing! That was the answer! Sure, it says on page 35, just pull down this pendant and that pendant as the halyards are slacked away. Oh, but they don't tell you about closing the hatches first. My leg still hurts.

CHAPTER 43

Signal: "Your Unshippy Actions Are Embarrassing Me"

I AM THINKING about making a large sign that I can erect when entering or leaving our harbor. The sign will read, "Yes, I know my fenders are hanging overboard." Perhaps there should be a signal flag for this message. *Chapman's* is strangely silent on this matter, but if there is a flag for such twaddle as "My vessel is healthy and I request free pratique," it seems to me there should be one for everyday cruising needs.

Sailing is rife with ritualistic little niceties, some of which retain their practical basis, but there is a special breed of sailor more concerned with the niceties than with the object of the whole mad exercise. I like to think of these sailors as mandarins: They would rather be dismasted than commit an error of manners or etiquette. It must be a matter of grave embarrassment to such persons that both Herman Melville and Joseph Conrad employed the phrase, "knots per hour."

Don't get me wrong. I like things to be nautically correct, too, but the real world of sailing, especially living aboard and sailing a large old wooden barn of a boat, precludes perfect conformity to the baroque etiquette of a gentler time. If I were to "make" eight bells every evening, I would probably be the object of general scorn and several shouts of "knock it off!" from other boats, not to mention CONTENT herself. As to those fenders (and anyone who calls them "bumpers" is wrong but may be a decent and worthwhile human being nevertheless), they hang overboard when I'm leaving the dock because I'm too busy trying to miss potential victims to take them in, and they hang overboard when I'm coming back in because I know that shortly I shall be too busy trying to maneuver for a glancing impact to mess with fenders. So I get them over early and brave the disapproval of the mandarins.

How do I know that the mandarins disapprove? That's easy: I'm something of a mandarin myself, you see. When I see someone charging along festooned with dangling fenders, saying "knots per hour," and committing other sins too horrible to catalogue, part of me sniffs, "dear, dear, how unshippy." I am saved from my own

120

condemnation of mandarins, however, because another part of me says, "Come off it, hot shot; get back on course." I am also saved from that condemnation because anything that I do is about 90% OK right up front because it's me doing it.

One of the burdens to be borne by anyone presuming to ownership of an old classic gaffer is the necessity, at least according to the mandarins, of being perfectly correct, nautically, all the time. Of course, that's not possible, and the attempt to live up to that goal is futile and probably bad for the liver. That's why we play fast and loose with many of the rules aboard CONTENT; also, it's a way of thumbing our nose at the spirit of nautical rectitude. That's why sometimes it's "downstairs" and "kitchen" and even "rope," aboard CONTENT.

We've recently returned from a cruise to Martha's Vineyard and points between there and Stamford, and we saw that the farther east we went the more flags we saw on sailing yachts. There were owner's flags and yacht ensigns and burgees and private signals and gosh sakes who knows what-all. We felt positively naked because we were flagless, unless you count a national flag of Denmark and a large red flag with "Condon Marine Hardwoods" on it. I got that one off the end of a load of white oak but I won't tell where.

Now, I allowed to Nancy as how we ought to get us some flags, too, so we could display them, but she observed that if we got the flags we'd have to learn how to fly them. From the peak? Truck? Leech? Jackstaff? Underway? Not underway? Sundown? Strike at sundown? Eight bells?—Enough! I quickly backed away from the awful responsibility of getting it all right. Suppose someone should see me with a flag flown on the wrong alternate Thursday? That plus my *bumpers* overboard would alienate me from mankind.

However, closer inspection of many of these beflagged boats showed that there's just as much fast and loose playing about with flag etiquette aboard other boats as there may be aboard CONTENT. For instance, one rule of displaying the yacht ensign seems to be, at least in many cases, "The yacht ensign shall be flown from anywhere until it rots off." I think I could get the hang of that after a while. So, old CONTENT may have some nondescript flags soon, as she continues happily on her unsteady course, slightly down by the head, stays'l luff not fully taut. But don't let me catch *your* boat in such disarray; that would be lubberly.

CHAPTER 44

Good Old Boat

I HAVE ALWAYS detested sentimentality, unless of course it is my own, in which case it is evidence of a fine and noble soul. I think that there's something about living aboard old CONTENT that breeds it. Even inanimate objects soon become targets of a kind of dewy-eyed regard aboard the old leaker. Not every object is so regarded, but some are, and I can't discern any general rule for predicting which objects will remain lifeless and which will become "good old this" and "good old that."

For instance, there's a pipe, a plain nondescript aluminum pipe, about a foot long, that we use as a boarding step when getting aboard from the dinghy. We shove the pipe into the bilge pump outlet, leaving about six inches protruding. It makes a handy step. If we were to lose this pipe overboard, my wife would cry and I would have to dive for it if recovery were even remotely possible. I would probably pretend to be reluctant to dive, but I know that I too would be saddened by the loss of our "good old pipe."

It made the transition from pipe to good old pipe on our passage to Connecticut from the Chesapeake, some six years ago. It had been a lumpy go, not because of wind but because of commercial traffic off the New Jersey coast. Indeed, we were mildly pooped by the stern wave of the TOYOTA MARU in Ambrose Channel, as she made her way, dead slow, to the dealerships of the New World. When we got to Milford, Connecticut, after five days of such rolling, I remembered the pipe. I had forgotten to take it out of the outlet hole after we had climbed aboard in the Chesapeake. I dashed to the side of the boat merely as a reflex, not expecting, even remotely, that the pipe would still be in place. Of course, there it was, as if we had been sitting at a mooring in a mill pond all that time. I reached down and grabbed what had suddenly become our "good old pipe." I felt as though the pipe itself had owed its survival to some special pipely virtue. I thought, "You're a hell of a pipe, you good old pipe," but I didn't say it—there are excesses of sentimentality that even I will not commit. Ever since, we have nurtured, cared for, worried about, and kept conscientious track of the whereabouts and well-being of our pipe—our good old pipe.

We may sail away from our anchorage with our fenders over the side, sheets in the water, but woe to anyone who forgets to take the good old pipe inboard. A friend once suggested that we get one of those yachtsy boarding ladders so we wouldn't have to contend with that "crummy pipe." We had him stoned to death in the market square.

Many other objects that were employed by the previous owner have been dispensed with without a qualm, so we are not merely becoming sentimental about anything that was on the boat when we took possession of her. Take the former owner's old seaboot socks, for instance. He had a sock lashed firmly around each of the four skylight opening jack handles, so he wouldn't hurt his head on them.

As soon as I came aboard I removed them, reasoning that I would rather suffer a few bumps on the head than put up with the ultimate in unshippy decor. I further reasoned that after a period of painful knocks, I would soon learn to avoid the handles. Little did I reckon with the ability of humans to adapt to trying circumstances. I did not learn to avoid the handles. I learned to bear cranial pain like a 12th-century Samurai. But there are no socks on our skylight handles.

Just to confuse matters, however, there is another sock-encased object that has been aboard ever since we took over from the previous owner and that object has indeed become further swathed in a sticky coating of sentimentality. It is a block of wood about a foot long that we use to prop open the foredeck hatch. Yes, I know, there are special fittings made for that sort of thing, but a block of wood wrapped in an old boot sock is the style aboard CONTENT. Why the sock? The former owner had two cats; we have two cats. When the cats knock the block off the little shelf underneath the hatch, it could hurt someone if not cushioned in the thick, fuzzy boot sock. Or, when CONTENT is rolling at anchor in an open roadstead, the block sometimes falls off. Instead of making a terrible clatter, it makes a comforting dull thud on the cabin sole. One hears that thud at 0300 and says, "It's nothing, just the hatch block . . . good old block."

Heaven knows how such a mundane object has achieved such a degree of sentimental regard, but it has, there's no doubt about it.

The other day my good seawife got out the ditty bag. Now, on most boats, that would be a sign that something shippy was about to happen, a line to be whipped, a cringle served. But no . . . aboard CONTENT on *this* occasion it meant that the hatch block sock was in need of darning. And so it was lovingly stitched back to health. Hell, that's more attention than *my* socks ever get aboard this packet!

CHAPTER 45

Steer Small and Damn Yer Eyes

JUST AS NO man is a hero to his valet, no man is skipper to his son. My son Jamey, for instance, is certain that CONTENT's continued state of positive buoyancy and my continued survival are just more mysteries of the universe—like the origin of the Easter Island statues or what happened to the key to the deck fitting for the water tank. When I ask him how come I've stayed afloat for so many years—if I'm so dumb—he begins to enumerate incidents involving my rescue by others. That makes me pout. I've been rescued often, but only rarely when I really *had* to be rescued; I'm just gracious about accepting offers of aid. Hell, I could have gotten myself off those flats in the Toogoodoo River in the Inland Waterway; it's just that winter was coming.

I suppose I have only myself to blame, though. Like Dr. Frankenstein, I have created my own monster. In an attempt to give my son confidence, I have overshot the mark and unwittingly convinced him of his infallibility. I have been too supportive. I should have ridiculed him more. Now it's too late to be rotten.

It all started when I first took Jamey sailing. He was about nine months old—no older, because I distinctly remember that I knew more than he did back then. We were aboard our little Pennant class sloop—wooden, of course—and there was a sharp little Northeaster coming down from the fog factory of New England. Long Island Sound had a lump of a sea running, and I put the monster below because I was afraid that sitting in the cockpit would scare him.

We were bounding along, close-hauled, and making quite a thrash out of it. Occasionally, I'd glance below to make sure the monster wasn't getting scared. Snug in the leeward bunk, he seemed to be having a fine time. Finally, a gust slammed into the sail, we heeled violently, and I had to round up to keep the little sloop on her feet. I thought, "That did it; now he'll be terrified," and looked below, prepared to see the kid in tears.

What I saw was a nine-month-old sea dog looking like a caricature of a character from a Jack London novel. Jamey was kneeling on one knee while the other leg was extended, braced against the mast. One hand was clenched around a grab rail in the overhead, while the other clenched his bottle of milk. His head was tilted back, the bottle thrust into his mouth. Despite our violent rolling and pitching, the kid's body remained vertical, as he compensated with legs, trunk, and one arm. Add 20 years, change the milk to Barbados rum, and you'd have an illustration for *The Sea Wolf*. I won't ask you to believe that he said, "Steer small, damn your eyes!" but it wouldn't have surprised me.

I should have recognized the signs of impending trouble right then. In a few years, after we got CONTENT, he was running up the rigging and sliding down the peak halyard just to show off. If I cautioned him, he would reply, "Don't worry about it, Dad," in a tone that I suppose exasperated English gentility used in speaking to dull-witted footmen.

This attitude of natural superiority soon became a source of great frustration to me. Before Jamey consented to be our son, I used to fantasize about having a son and teaching him sailorly lore. You know—the old sailor teaches the boy how to tie a bowline. The old sailor teaches the boy how to read a chart. You've seen it a hundred times in 19th-century paintings. The old sailor is handsomely old and weather-beaten. The boy's expression is one of rapt attention and affection for the old sailor.

Aboard CONTENT, that's not the way it happens at all. It's like this: you take a piece of line and you say, "Jamey, let me show you how to tie a bowline." The rotten little creep's eyes roll heavenward, there is a bored sigh, and he says, "I know all that, Dad." If he doesn't say that, he announces that *Star Wars* begins in about 20 minutes and he really doesn't have much time for knots.

The really unforgivable part of it is that he really *does* know. I don't know how; God knows he's never allowed *me* to teach him anything, but somehow he has learned knots, chart reading, ship handling, sail setting—brain surgery, I suppose—you name it, all of which he demonstrates with a skill that I find intolerable. If I find the fink who has been teaching my son behind my back, the fur's gonna fly.

This unfortunate situation does have its advantages, though—or at least one advantage. It helps to identify CONTENT to strangers. After all, I daresay there are other boats named CONTENT, other gaff-rigged pilot cutters, even others with cats walking around on the bowsprit. But how many others are co-skippered by a 13-year-old who knows everything and an oaf who needs to be reminded not to step on his fingers when coming up the companionway?

I know this uniqueness has served as an identifier on at least one occasion. We had been coming down the Inland Waterway in company with another boat and, characteristically, had fallen behind. Our friend had anchored some miles ahead to wait, and had been questioning passing vessels about our whereabouts. "Did you pass a big white gaff-rigged cutter named CONTENT?" he would yell. Not everyone can see our name on the transom, so there was quite a bit of ambiguity. Many people thought they might have seen such a boat, but weren't sure. Finally, my friend's doubts were allayed. To his question about seeing "a big white cutter . . . etc.," a passing boatman replied, "Oh, do you mean that old boat with the kid who was in charge of everything?" My friend knew the passing skipper had seen none other than CONTENT.

So, if any readers have questions about wooden boats, or anything at all, just write to me. I'll ask Jamey.

CHAPTER 46

The Old and the New

I HAVE NEVER thought of myself as a purist in this psychiatric ward that comprises the world of wooden boats. More than once have I pointed out that were it not for technological advances in large-molecule chemistry, especially the chemistry of really stinky stuff, I probably never would have been able to sleep in a dry bunk. As things are, thanks to modern chemistry, I can often find a sleeping position that manages to allow me to miss the truly sodden places in my bunk. So, I have often championed the practical virtues of some modern, stinky product or other.

However, their traditional counterparts are, almost without exception, aesthetically superior. In the matter of smell, for instance, contrast the experience of inhaling in a shop where a wooden boat is being planked up with, say, cedar, and inhaling, if you dare, in a shop where they are laying up a boat with fiberglass. There is something healthy about the smell of wood shavings, but fiberglass resin doesn't even have a smell that belongs on this planet. It's a smell that is totally *alien*. I'm not talking about smelling good versus smelling bad. CONTENT's kitty litter box don't smell like no roses, Mac, but there's nothing *alien* about it.

This was all brought home to me recently when I tripped over a container of pine tar that I've had on deck for more than two years. I use it for the standing rigging and . . . and . . . well, gosh—sometimes when I get to feelin' low I just go over and smell that pine tar. It smells like pine. It's wholesome. It's not only wholesome, but it preserves both wire and rope rigging and apparently has an infinite shelf life.

By contrast, the bedding compound that I had been looking for when I tripped over the pine tar was completely alien; it had an extraterrestrial smell to it, and whatever its shelf life had been, I had certainly bought it too late. I remember inserting the cartridge into the caulking gun ("cartridge" . . . "gun" . . . even the terms connected with this modern stuff are intimidating), puncturing the plastic membrane sealer (these glop cartridges are all designed by Sigmund Freud), and squeezing the handle of the gun. Nothing happened. In desperation I cut open the cartridge. The stuff had changed into something that I would rather not remember, let alone describe. It was . . . *alien.*

The point is that traditional bedding compounds, and certainly pine tar, not only do the job but are friendlier to mankind. In the old days, bedding compound tended to separate into a solid and liquid component, especially after long storage, but you could always reconstitute it by working the solids back into solution. It took patience and several broken stirring sticks, but it could be done—and the damn stuff looked, smelled, and even felt as though it had its origins on this planet. In fact, it often reminded me of the way peanut butter used to separate out before the days of homogenized everything.

CONTENT provides an especially good vantage point from which to think of these matters because hidden within her old bones are the boat maintenance materials of several decades. I can compare the properties of deck caulking from 1930 to those of, say, 1960, and I can tell you this much: None of the damn stuff really works, but there is an important difference. The oakum, cotton, and tar of the more remote past can be removed with a conventional reefing tool. The only thing that will remove the various plastics or polysulfides or whatever they're called is a circular power saw and the will of God.

There is something infuriatingly ironic about seam glop that allows water to pour through and yet clings with maniacal tenacity to the sides of the seam. And when traditional materials quit working, at least they're honest about it. They say, "See, we're dried out, no good, you can practically wipe us out with your bent file tang." The polyglop says, "We may be no good for keeping water out, but we're still good enough to keep you from getting rid of us."

When traditional materials are dead they have the good grace to look and behave accordingly. I know *people* who don't have that much sense.

CHAPTER 47

"Progress" Viewed with Grave Suspicion

I HAVE DISCOVERED the basic human urge—or, at least, the basic sailor's urge—and it is not the desire for sex, power, or even food. It is the desire to complicate. I have just been going through several boating magazines and wondering why I wasn't interested in most of the contents. The reason is that there's not much in them about boats. What is there is lots of stuff about machinery, something called "performance," and instrumentation. Incidentally, the instrumentation is all "state-of-the-art" and can interface with other instrumentation. (I think this means that when the electronic knotmeter goes haywire, so does the damn autopilot.)

At the risk of repeating myself, I repeat myself: I am not, as I've said in previous polemics, against progress. But fixing what ain't broke ain't progress. For instance, anchor winches are good; it's easier to weigh anchors with them. Wind-direction indicators are silly. It's no easier to tell wind direction with them. In fact, they create the least trouble when they are broken—which is almost always. When they are working they gyrate wildly as the boat rolls, and the skipper must mentally average out the wild swings of the indicator. And then, all he has is the relative wind at the masthead, the one place on the boat where he has no sail area.

My alternative is ingenious. Try to stay with me on this: you turn your face directly into the wind. When your face is facing directly into the wind, the wind is coming from the direction in which your face is facing. True, you have only the relative wind at face height above the deck, but that's a lot better than at the masthead, and your face didn't cost $279.95; you got it free as a standard accessory, and it works almost all the time.

I believe that racing enthusiasts are most likely to succumb to the received dogma that instruments can do it better than people. Cruising sailors tend not to be as exacting as racers. A few degrees to port or to starboard of the ideal course, for instance, is not as likely to make them antisocial. Also, they are poorer, not as likely to spring for an electronic compass, say, that "senses the Earth's magnetic field" thousands of times per second to an accuracy within one degree, as one product's promotion puts it.

The irony is that the less demanding approach may well yield just as good or even superior accuracy, and we all know how important one degree accuracy is when steering a boat. Most of us already have an instrument that, in fact, senses the Earth's magnetic field an infinite number of times per second—it's called a magnetic compass. As a matter of fact, a good one does that with much better accuracy than one degree. Of course, no helmsman can steer that well. Only people criticizing the helmsman can do that.

The answer to all this is, of course, that such an instrument is not intended to interface with people; it's supposed to interface with the autopilot. The *autopilot* is what steers with such superhuman accuracy—as long as the weather remains mild, of course. In severe weather, one guards against excessive battery drain or autopilot "hunting" by tuning down the sensitivity, which allows the autopilot to do a very sensible thing: steer like a human being—an unskillful one, to be sure, but whaddya want for $2,000?

The urge to high-tech-it-up seems, to me, to stem from a deep-seated feeling of inferiority—perhaps justified, in some cases—but, in the interest of being nice, I won't pursue that line of inquiry. Many of us feel that anything done by a little black box must be done better than a plain old human can do. That may be true in many cases; but, strangely, it's not, I think, often true on boats. The human nose, for instance, can detect gasoline fumes more sensitively than the best bilge "sniffer," and the human ear can synchronize two engine rpms about as well as any thingamajig obtained from some nautical boutique.

Maybe the trend began with pushbutton telephones. For decades mankind had to laboriously move that heavy dial around by finger power alone. Now we can push buttons, saving .06 microcalories per digit dialed. God, what a relief! Then, we were so pleased with our success that the same methods of fixing what ain't broke went to sea. If my theory is correct, it wouldn't be the first time that a disease of civilization had infected the seagoing world. My cure is to view with grave suspicion any piece of gear that cannot be understood by simply looking at it carefully. That doesn't include sails, of course; no one knows how they work.

CHAPTER 48

Bowsprit Envy

U NTIL THIS MOMENT I've never taken the Freudian view of things very seriously, preferring to remember what the great Viennese himself is supposed to have said, "Usually, a telephone pole is a telephone pole." However, I have just finished running CONTENT's 10-foot bowsprit inboard. There she sits, a "bald-headed" boat—no bowsprit. I feel as if there's something wrong, something . . . well . . . *missing*. I keep telling myself that a bowsprit is only a bowsprit, but another voice (and it sounds like Mae West) says, "Come up and see me some time, when you've shipped your bowsprit."

Oh well, I'm probably just overreacting to a recent blow to my self-esteem (a chronically fragile thing, to begin with). After all, boat people are somewhere between bag ladies and organ grinders in social prestige. This blow came in a letter sent to me by the new owners of the boatyard where I used to keep CONTENT. Yes, used to. It seems that the new owners did not want certain types of boats in their boatyard. Now, that's OK by me; if a guy buys a boatyard and decides he wants only green boats in his yard, then you either paint your boat green or get the hell out of the man's yard. But there was nothing so concrete in this letter. It contained portentous phrases such as, "We have examined your boat. . . ."

Now, why does that send shivers down my spine? Why do I hear that phrase spoken with a German accent by a man with a monocle? The gist of the letter was, "We have examined your boat; get out." The implications are clear enough. CONTENT, under examination, had not passed. Had she been better, a Cal-40 perhaps, she might have passed her examination and the letter would have said, "We have examined your boat and are overcome by her magnificence. Please stay in our yard until it shall be your gracious pleasure to leave."

But more than CONTENT's not measuring up, I know that it is I myself who didn't measure up. Perhaps if I had been a better human being, more of a *man*. . . . (Good God! Was it that my CONTENT's bowsprit was too small?) Nonsense, this whole affair is only about CONTENT, not about me—right? Nevertheless, CONTENT is only wood and bronze. It is I who am responsible for her. "We have examined your boat," indeed. You mean you have examined *me*, my wife, my cats, my taste in music, art, literature, my serum cholesterol, the totality of my *being*, you cross-grained, gimlet-eyed bunch of tofu-eating, upwardly mobile market analysts!

And on top of all that, I lose my bowsprit. I mean, CONTENT's, of course; and it isn't lost, it's retracted. Good Lord, the more I explain this, the worse it sounds. Perhaps I'd better just stick to the facts. Having been ejected (more Freudian grist) from my old home, I have moved CONTENT across the river to a yard that did not examine me/CONTENT first. No doubt, when they get around to it, I shall have to wear a bell around my neck and cry, "unclean!" as I shuffle along, assuming they let me stay at all.

Ah, but I go too far. Actually, the yard I now occupy seems quite congenial. Why should it not? For, on my first day here, it seemed that half the former population of my original yard, including employees, had preceded me here. So, it seems that I have not been singled out for a putdown. Rather, a whole slew of us ne'er-do-wells and drifters have been "examined" and found wanting.

Why doesn't this make me feel better? I'll tell you why. Not only have I been examined and found inadequate (Heard about poor old Kasanof? Retracted his bowsprit, you know), but I'm not even *unique*! Just an unremarkable example of a whole class of shmoes who don't measure up. It's all reminiscent of that day Miss Hoffnagle tapped one on the shoulder during the singing of *America the Beautiful* and pronounced one a "listener," not a "singer."

Even the foreshortening, withdrawal, and retraction of my bowsprit have disreputable overtones in addition to obvious pornographic significance. It was done, you see, for no good seamanlike reason. It had nothing to do with the "winter rig" common among working sail on the English coast. No, running in the bowsprit may reduce sail area, shift the center of effort aft, and all that nautical stuff, but it also accomplished something else not mentioned in handbooks of yacht design. At 40 cents a foot per day for wet storage (while working on the boat), the "winter rig" saves me about 150 clams a month.

So there CONTENT sits, a "baldheaded" boat perhaps for the first time in her life, just so her owner can save a few miserable bucks. It all seems too crass, I know. But crass is what is going to allow me to come up with the bucks for the next phase of CONTENT's repair, her hull. Sister frames, new sheerstrakes, bulwarks, floor timbers, refastening . . . all await. Believe it or not, I'm looking forward to it. After a year of fooling with plywood and, yes, fiberglass, it will feel good to get back to real wood again. In fact, it will feel so good that just thinking about it makes me want to run my bowsprit out prematurely.

CHAPTER 49

An Illness So Unlovely

THERE IS NO such thing as chronic seasickness. Everyone gets over it. All the "cures" work and none of them work. It's like the rain dance. Every rain dance in recorded history has been followed by rain. (I cannot forbear observing that rain dances are never done in the dry season.) I think that that is the point of the sailor's old joke: The only sure-fire cure for seasickness is to go to sleep under an apple tree.

Nevertheless, I do not believe that the malady is completely out of our control. Seasickness is controlled by something, I am certain. Unfortunately, it may be something in the area of the supernatural such as in the case of electrolysis or marine insurance.

In my own case, seasickness has never struck me on my own boat. It has never occurred when it would have caused a real hazard to safety, at night, for instance, or when (as used to happen not infrequently in my youth) I was the only sober person on the boat. It has never happened on a wooden boat—well, almost never.

From the above, one might conclude that seasickness is psychosomatic. Only someone who has never seen a seasick dog could believe that. I have read a description of seasick horses aboard a Navy transport during the Second World War. Horses with a psychosomatic illness? Not even if they were from California.

My own experience with seasickness indicates that there's something very real at work, but in accordance with some unknown principle in addition to two preconditions: You must be on a boat, and the water must be at least not dead flat.

Although I do not get sick easily, it has happened. Although almost all of my sailing has been in wooden boats, only once have I been seasick on one—and even then, one might say that I asked for, even deserved, what I got.

We had been sailing in rough weather looking for a light tower that had once again drifted off station (unlikely, I admit, but what other explanation is there?). I was dining from a can of cold smoked oysters and a jar of martini onions when I dropped my fork into the bilge. While fishing for it in the black diesel-laden water, I overheard my skipper ask where I was and then loudly speculate that I was probably wasting all those good smoked oysters.

I knew he was teasing, because he knew that I was one of those people who "never get seasick." To turn the jest back on him, I began to imitate the sounds appropriate to the clinical condition under discussion. It had the desired effect. He began to plead in terror, "Not in the bilge, for God's sake! "

I had planned to appear on deck smiling, apparently relieved and uncaring about the legacy I had left in the bilge. But fate decreed otherwise. My imitation sickness suddenly became real. I staggered topside just in time to make it to the lee rail. For years afterward, the skipper swore that I had begun my eruption in his bilge and that he hadn't been able to deodorize the boat for weeks. Naturally, he never went for my "It all started as a joke" story. Neither would I, if our roles had been reversed.

As to the cures, I have probably heard most of them, from the "Stay on deck" to the "Go below and sleep it off" schools of thought. I don't think it matters, but I do think it helps to tell the sufferer something, on the great chicken-soup principle. This tells the victim that you are concerned and sorry that he or she is unwell. It doesn't matter that your concern is that he may befoul the teak or that the illness is so unlovely in its main manifestations that it may communicate itself to you.

Then there is an entire class of cures focused on smelling various things. Orange peel is a popular item. Well, orange peel smells good, and I suppose I'd rather be nauseated and smelling orange peel than nauseated and not smelling orange peel.

There is the sadistic method of cures in which the theory is to induce the sufferer to upchuck as quickly as possible. There may be something to that, but I believe it is practiced mainly for the entertainment of crewmembers who are inordinately proud of the fact that they are not seasick.

Although I've said there are no cures, I always tell people to fix their eyes on the horizon and to try not to observe the boat. I explain that this helps the brain relate what the eyes are seeing to what the inner ear canals are telling it about the kinesthetic sensation due to the boat's motion. This, of course, is pure speculation at best and utter claptrap at worst (or maybe the other way around), but it does accomplish one thing: With one more pair of eyes on the horizon, you're more likely to spot light towers that have gone adrift.

CHAPTER 50

Seeing Your Learning Curve in Wood

I'VE JUST COME to the conclusion that it can be a dreadful mistake for the amateur wooden boat "carpenter" to step back and look at his handiwork before filler and paint have accomplished their primary function: hiding the goofs. Just do the job without looking at it, and then, as quickly as possible, cover up what you've done with something opaque. Otherwise, you may find yourself in the same position I found myself in recently: yearning to go back in time and begin the job again, now that I had developed some skill. That's the trouble with us amateurs. By the time we finally learn how to do a job, it is done—and we will probably never have a chance to do that particular job again.

In my case, the matter is made even worse because I can see (and I'm sure the casual observer can see) the history of my learning process right there in the wood. The laminated sheerstrake on the starboard side starts out sloppy aft and gets better as I move forward. Port side, the trend continues . . . until, up around the chainplates, the job borders on acceptable (that is, the "What the hell, it'll look OK once it's painted" level). There's even a spot, about two feet long, where two laminates fit the way they're supposed to, so that the line between them is all but invisible. Does that lessen the dissatisfaction? No, it merely accents the imperfections all around it. Giving a starving man one bit of roast duck doesn't quell his hunger pangs.

Maybe a solution would be to find a derelict boat to hone your skills on, before attempting to do some non-trivial carpentry on a wooden boat. Make your mistakes on the practice boat. Isn't that why fledgling surgeons first practice on animals?

Of course, I admit that some amateurs seem to be able to get it right the first time. I believe there are a number of reasons for this, the first being that they are not amateurs. The guy doing such a neat job of soldering or welding turns out to be a master welder. The fellow making a beautiful grating is a professional cabinetmaker. Or perhaps they've done the job many times before, even though they are amateurs. I'm pretty good at splicing broken masts because I once sailed a Star. I'm not too bad at working with copper sheathing because CONTENT finds shoals with the enthusiasm of a cow smelling out a salt lick. Finally, most people have boats that are . . . well . . . not eccentric.

Here's what I mean by that: Things that work on one boat will usually work on another. For instance, if you have a template for a starboard frame, you can usually use it for the port-side frame. But not on CONTENT, you can't. She's not symmetrical on either side of her long axis. I'm not talking about *subtle* here. Subtle would be standing on the crosstrees, looking down and saying, "I wonder if she's quite symmetrical." No, I'm talking about standing on the crosstrees, looking down and saying, "Good God!"

Most boats head into the wind when at anchor. CONTENT almost never does. Worse than that, she seems to find a compromise between the force of the wind and of the current, and to do this she does quite a bit of sailing at her mooring. This eccentricity once gave me a good illustration of how proven methods have a way of not working on CONTENT. On one of her wayward sailing expeditions she had annihilated about four feet of rubrail on a boat that I had anchored too close to—that is to say, within sight of. I had found the damage before the other skipper had returned, and instead of bugging out in accordance with accepted maritime practices, I had left my name, address, and telephone number in his cockpit, offering either my money or my services as (I blush to say it) a "skilled carpenter."

He took me up on the latter option, and I fixed his rubrail perfectly. Just recently, I had to do a similar job on CONTENT, only easier. I had to scarf two pieces of oak for a caprail. The surfaces to be joined met perfectly, I applied the epoxy as I had a thousand times before, and the joint held . . . for about a month. One day, after a heavy rain, it popped open. All of a sudden, epoxy didn't work anymore. Maybe the rain had something to do with it. Maybe epoxy should only be used in the Egyptian Sudan.

I'm sure readers will have many explanations for this failure, but I already know the reason. CONTENT is just . . . strange. What can you expect of a boat that is lopsided and sticks her stern up into the wind like a mule in a rainstorm?

I foolishly announced previously that I was going to restore CONTENT's tumblehome. She must have heard me. You remember my cautioning against looking at your work? One of the things I noticed when I took that overall gander at my new sheerstrake was that it lay exactly where the old one had lain. Nor was I able to pull it in to the frames as I had planned. Don't ask me how this could happen; confound it, it just happened. It's CONTENT.

I have a suspicion that perhaps even the original builders were unable to pull the original five-quarter pine planks in as they had intended. That's what can happen when a boat is "eyed up," rather than lofted from a table of offsets. CONTENT's shape certainly suggests that either she was eyed up or perhaps the lines were faired by a loftsman with astigmatism. At any rate, from now on I shall affect the confident air of a carpenter who just "eyes her up." That way, if something doesn't come out right, I can claim that it's the way I wanted it from the start. That's an amateur skill I may be pretty good at already.

CHAPTER 51

Identifying Lumberyard Wood

WOODENBOAT MAGAZINE has published several articles on wood technology and I have read them all with great interest, but, like most technical articles, they tend to get a bit high-brow. Reading too much of this stuff may mislead the unwary into thinking that wood is a complex, ever-changing organic material. This may be true, but it is counter to the mental health of the wooden boat sailor to dwell on this unfortunate fact.

For those of us who deal with wood as a primary engine of financial doom, it suffices to know that there are only two basic types of wood, and we are concerned in this monograph with only one of these. There is hardware-store wood and lumberyard wood; we are concerned with the latter.

It is easy to distinguish between these types. Hardware-store wood looks nice, is light in color and weight, and is relatively soft. It is sold by men and women, some of whom are under age 50 and have names like Skip and Kimberly. (I know this because they wear name tags.) Lumberyard wood, on the other hand, looks hairy and sometimes has the bark still on it. It is usually somewhat darker in color, always heavier in weight, and is relatively hard. It is sold only by men over 50 named either Gus or Al. (I know this because they often yell at each other. They never wear name tags because they don't give a damn whether you know their names or not.)

The different types of lumberyard wood are easily identified and their properties for boatbuilding just as easily understood. Let us consider them in no particular order.

Boatyard Wood

This wood is found lying about in boatyards. It is usually gray in color, warped, cracked, and generally not worth stealing unless it has been fabricated into a ladder. In that case, "borrowed" is the accepted term, although such borrowing often takes place when only the borrower is present. Some boatyard wood is found in the shape of staging. Such wood is gray and checked and split, like most boatyard wood, but can be readily identified as material intended to

provide safe footing for those working at considerable height. Iden-
tification of staging is confirmed if one observes a pronounced twist
in the plank. This ensures that the plank can rock violently as one attempts to walk on it. That rocking action discourages complacency
on the part of the worker, a prime cause of boatyard accidents.

Bilge Wood

This wood is found only in the bilges of wooden boats. It is black
and smells like diesel oil. Frames, floors, and knees are made of bilge
wood, although bilge trees are becoming quite scarce because of
rapid deforestation of our national timber stands and, for all I know,
the overharvesting of the blue whale.

Mast Wood

Mast wood is of two types: round or rectangular cross section. Either type may be hollow or solid but not both. Hollow mast wood
allows the designer to run the fall of halyards down inside the mast,
thus making it absolutely impossible to silence the halyards by pre-
venting them from slapping against the inside of the mast. Solid
masts were invented to solve this problem, but solid mast trees are
becoming as scarce as bilge trees.

Pretty Wood

This wood is generally found on the inside of boats owned by people with good taste. Such people do not have cups that say "Galley
Slave" on one and "Captain" on the other. They do not have
Formica table tops, and they do not eat cold Hormel chili out of the
can. They make me very uncomfortable, these people. A significant
amount of pretty wood is a type of cedar commonly found in the
Caribbean and consequently called Philippine mahogany. This wood
is popular in boat interiors because it is brittle, easily split, and yet
soft enough to dent easily.

Fake Wood

This wood is a close relative of pretty wood in that most of it is
pretty, at least on one side. Fake wood may be a veneer, a plywood,
or a composition made by mashing up perfectly good wood and then
scrunching it all together again with a lot of glue. Why bust it up if
you're only going to stick it back together again, you may ask? Because it's more expensive and can be turned out in great sheets. Fake

wood is easy to identify because it either looks like something else or like nothing at all. So, if you see something that looks like wood only has no grain, it's probably fake wood.

Hint: Only people who eat cold Hormel chili from the can utilize fake wood. If they eat their chili with a plastic spoon, they're my kind of folks.

CHAPTER 52

Boatyard Etiquette

THE OTHER DAY, as I slithered yet again underneath my boat, the melancholy thought occurred that I had been slithering under one boat or another in various boatyards for the past four decades or so—and still had an undetermined number of days of slithering ahead of me with little to show for it. After all, 40 years is time enough to build several boats, plant and harvest a pine forest, or research and write the definitive biography of Vlad the Impaler. And what have I accomplished in the same period? Well, I can slither real good and can get through spaces that would stymie a weasel.

Maybe I'm too hard on myself. All that "messing about in boats" has at least taught me something about boatyard etiquette. I don't mean obvious stuff like never being too friendly with the guy in the next boat (he may want to borrow something). I'm talking fine points here.

For instance, if you don't want something to be stolen and you find it inconvenient to put it on deck, put it well under your boat, preferably right underneath the keel. There seems to be an invisible moral force field surrounding boats that are hauled out. It repels casual gear thieves. However, this field grows ineffective with distance from its source; a screwdriver left 20 feet from its owner's boat is exactly four times more likely to be stolen than one left 10 feet away. High school physics students will instantly recognize the inverse-square law. Obviously the Anti-Thief Field is strongest right underneath the boat, but a really determined thief or a personal friend can overcome it. Also, the ATF is negatively phototropic; that is, it's degraded by sunlight. If a tool has been left within a boat's shadow, it is less likely to be stolen than the same tool left the same distance away but in sunlight.

Power tools are less likely to be stolen than hand tools, probably because they are plugged in and would-be thieves aren't sure where the receptacle is for that particular tool, especially when surrounded by a bird's nest of power cords. The etiquette of the electrical power outlet is a dicey one, though. Skippers of very large yachts (or their professional captains) believe they have a divine right to all receptacles within a quarter-mile of the yacht. And skippers of steel boats of *any* size believe the same thing.

Now, you probably don't want to start calling these butt-heads names right away, so here are some non-confrontational methods for dealing with butt-heads. First, remember "an ounce of prevention." If you see an empty receptacle near your boat, plug something into it, even if it's a rotisserie. This is like establishing squatter's rights. Once you're there, it's harder to dislodge you.

If all the receptacles are taken when you arrive, and there's no one in sight on the offending boat, just unplug something and see who yells. It may well be some poor bastard six boats down the line who just knocked out all the power in his part of the yard by plugging in with everything turned on aboard his gin palace. That's why, when performing a blind unplugging, it is well to avoid all "twist-lock" plugs, especially those attached to power cords larger than your wrist. Be especially wary of cords that are warm or hot to the touch or which are apparently disrupting the flight paths of migratory birds.

Ladders are a big problem in boatyards. There is a law of nature that causes the number of ladders available to be one less than the number of boats that need them. This produces a never ending game of musical ladders. Some people tie their ladders to their boats, and that is a psychological deterrent. It's one thing to walk off with a ladder; it's quite another to climb it, untie it, and then make off with it (although I can tell you that it's done). Hint: Tie up your ladder with a "baggage porter's bend" (you know, the one they use to attach a tag to your luggage), then take the free ends below decks somewhere and tie them. That forces a would-be ladder thief to enter your boat if he wants your ladder; most won't go that far. Alternatively, you could chain your ladder to the shrouds. I once did this by using my bicycle chain. You guessed it; somebody then stole my bicycle.

Now, there's a reverse side to most of this. Suppose you see a nice piece of hardwood lying around, and you don't know if it belongs to anyone. Suppose you really need both electrical receptacles. Suppose you need a ladder and can't find one not in use. My suggestion is gradualism. Gradually move the tempting piece of lumber closer and closer to your boat. As it gets nearer, the reverse action of the moral force field gradually makes it more and more your own property. Use all receptacles if you must, but use a "Y" connector on one so another person can also use it. If he needs more, let him supply the additional connector. But make sure you make him feel guilty about the possibility of overloading the circuit. After all, you were there first. As to the ladder, ask to borrow one, but don't return it at the promised time. Use it until the original users ask for its return. Then return it with profuse apologies.

Get the idea? It's niceties like these that can make the world a better place.

CHAPTER 53

Good Stuff

SOME MATERIALS are just plain nicer than others. I don't mean more useful or better in any objective way; I mean just plain nicer, friendlier to humans. To explain, take this example from the animal kingdom: All life on Earth higher than some primitive molds and lichens would not exist were it not for earthworms. Just the same, I'll take golden retrievers any day. They're just a whole bunch nicer. Yes, I know there's folks that get awful sentimental about their earthworms, but I just gotta tell it like I see it.

What brought on this observation was my recent completion (assuming I don't have to redo the damn job) of recaulking and coppering CONTENT from stem to mast below the waterline. After such an ordeal, you'd think I'd hate the sight of a copper nail or copper sheet. In fact, I just plain like the stuff. Copper is nice. It looks nice, feels nice, cuts easy, stays bent the way you want it bent, and costs no more per pound than beluga caviar.

Aluminum, on the other hand, is lighter, stronger, and has much wider application in the marine world than copper. I hate it. Cast aluminum gets those disgusting white pustules on it when wet. I think they're called "flowers" by machinists and metal workers. Flowers hell, I know pustules when I see them. If I had a horse with that stuff on it, I'd shoot it. Extruded or rolled aluminum won't bend the way you want it to, and it takes a real expert to weld it without having the plates warp like a piece of hog ear left too long on the skillet. Aluminum is just not a friendly material.

Note that each of these materials is a natural substance, so I'm not taking the well-worn granola-eating tree-hugger's line that everything natural is good and everything man-made is bad. Plenty of man-made stuff is good and plenty is bad.

Diesel fuel is nice. Gasoline is terrible. Maybe there's something wrong with my sensory organs, but I like the smell of diesel fuel and I even like the smell of a well-tuned diesel engine's exhaust. These smells are wholesome. I met a ship's engineer once who shared my olfactory peculiarity. He even added the following bit of medical advice: A cut will heal faster if dipped in clean diesel fuel. I tried it once

145

on one of my frequent wounds, and it seemed to work. Of course, I had nothing to compare it to, but the curative power of diesel is widely respected in the Dutch merchant marine, according to my informant, if that's any evidence in its favor.

I know that gasoline stings like hell, tastes lousy (my protective reflexes as a siphoner are slow), and smells like Vinnie's Jiffy Lube where all the "mechanics" are tattooed. Gasoline is also dangerously flammable, whereas, as every owner of a diesel stove knows, diesel fuel resists all but the most frantically determined efforts to ignite it.

Pine tar, sometimes called Stockholm tar, is something of a paradox. On objective grounds, it's wonderful stuff, of course. It's good for everything it touches—which is a damn lucky thing, because it touches everything. If you open a jug of pine tar on deck and begin working with it, within the hour there will be pine tar fingerprints at the masthead and on the best china in the galley. Three weeks after tarring your rigging, pine tar will still be dripping on your deck. (Make that four weeks, if your decks are teak.) It gets into everything, but it smells so good that it's hard to believe it doesn't do *some* good to anything it touches. I don't suppose that's really true. I certainly wouldn't want it on vanilla ice cream. Then again, I've never given it a fair try.

Fiberglass resin, on the other hand, is noxious stuff no matter how you look at it. I've recently learned that the damned stuff isn't even waterproof. That's no great sin in itself; heck, wood isn't waterproof, but at least it's not poisonous or carcinogenic and doesn't smell like landfill rejected by the city council of Love Canal. Besides, I just don't feel comfortable around any material that gets hot all by itself when you mix the two cans of glop together. It's against nature. In my view, stuff that gets hot should have a fire under it. If it doesn't, it's *chemistry*, and that's just a fancy way of saying that it smells real bad.

Iron is generally a friendly material, although one must have the right tools to work with it. When dipped in molten zinc it is quite hardy, as long as it is not exposed to seawater. With enough galvanized fastenings in the hull there's no need to attach sacrificial zincs. You already got 'em. Swedish black iron is extremely nice. I have not got the foggiest notion of what it is, but CONTENT's floors are made of this, according to her original survey, made I think at the end of the conquest of Gaul.

I know Swedish iron's good stuff because it has the name

"Swedish" in it. (Remember Stockholm tar?) In the world of wooden boats, anything Swedish or connected with that country is good. Not as good as Dutch, of course, but pretty damn good. I don't mean to show ethnic favoritism here. After all, the much-praised "Stockholm" tar is nothing but the pine tar used by the Greeks as they sailed for Troy. Hence, Homer's "black ships." Come to think of it, I bet that's the origin of retsina, that dreadful Greek wine with resin in it. Those poor bastards were tarring their rig and, as I've mentioned, the damn stuff gets into everything—and it got into their wine. Sailor-like, they wouldn't admit that it was a mistake, and for 3,000 years they've been drinking the stuff.

Another mystery solved!

CHAPTER 54

Predicting Weather

THERE HAS BEEN a great deal of nonsense written about the sailorly art of predicting the weather. Most of it is based on the view from a high school freshman physics lab. You remember: wet bulb this, dry bulb that, cumulonimbus, cold front—all that good stuff. The reason that none of this Boy Scout merit-badge palaver is ever really used at sea is because there are much simpler ways to go about it.

The main determining factors for making weather predictions are as follows: Where are you? What time of year is it? What time of day is it? What does NOAA say? This last is the least important, because research looking into a correlation between NOAA predictions and the actual weather has so far produced inconclusive results.

Here's the way my system works. If, for instance, you are sailing in Eastern Long Island Sound during the summer and it is late afternoon, you are in a flat calm and you will continue to be in this condition for the indefinite future. In addition, you'd better get your hook down somewhere soon, because as soon as the sun sets, you will be socked in by fog so thick you can walk home on it. There is a fog factory somewhere between Boston and New Haven that goes into high gear during the summer. As to NOAA, there's no need to listen. I can give you their prediction right now. Winds will be southeast at 10 to 15 knots (you only think you're becalmed), and there is a 70% chance of fog tonight. The reason I can give their prediction is that it is unvarying from June through August.

If you are sailing in that region during the winter, the report will have the wind at northeast, and there will be a lower probability of fog.

The state of your barometer is another good clue to weather prediction. If the glass is cloudy, there is moisture in the atmosphere. This sign generally appears when it is raining. If the condensation is on the inside of the glass, however, the moisture is inside the barometer, a fact of little predictive value except, of course, for weather inside the barometer.

A useful trick is to tap the barometer. This tells you if the cover glass is loose or if roaches are breeding behind the instrument. Some sailors have suggested that tapping may jar the pointer so that it will jump to the current pressure reading if the needle is stuck on the old one. I would suggest that if your barometer needle doesn't smoothly follow ambient pressure without being assaulted, it's time to get a new one or at least stop thumping on the one you've got. Hell, that's probably what mucked it up in the first place.

As to the actual barometer readings, forget 'em. More than a century ago, Capt. Fitzroy demonstrated these readings to be of little practical value by writing dozens of "rules" relating them to wind direction, velocity, and changes in these factors. The rules are so complicated that I have never known anyone who knows them by heart or who would ever dream of trying to apply them. We are left with the words "rainy," "change," and "fair" on the face of the barometer. If these had any practical utility, we could get along perfectly well without all the other rules, including old Fitzroy's.

Some mariners believe that the behavior of birds provides a clue to impending weather. I think there is something to this, but not much. It is thought that land birds seen flying toward shore are a predictor of approaching bad weather. I believe it is just as likely to signal approaching charter fishing boats. Alternatively, the damn birds may just be lost. If they were so smart, what are they doing out there over the water in the first place? And if they were merely blown offshore by a storm, why didn't their weather smarts warn them in time to hunker down under Ma Pritchard's woodshed? I do think that following birds may be a good idea, though. They may lead you to a charter boat, and you can ask the skipper what he thinks the weather is going to be.

Just remember to do the opposite of what he says. His main interest is in getting you to go away so you won't foul his lines with the keel of your "damn rag boat," and so that you won't see where the good fishing is. When he really wants to know what the weather is likely to do, he'll phone home to find out what the lady on CNN says.

We amateurs would do well to follow the lead of seasoned professional mariners.

CHAPTER 55

"Interesting, But Thank Goodness It's Not Ours!"

I'M NOT GENERALLY one to feel sorry for myself, but it's pretty hard for a feller to keep his little chin up when he realizes that he's been fired by his cat. I'm accustomed to people taking on an air of condescension about CONTENT and me. I'm aware that "You sure got a lot of work cut out for you" more often than not means, "You poor, dumb bastard." But to be fired by my own cat. . . . I thought stuff like that only happened to Rodney Dangerfield.

Ever since my good seawife and I had to move ashore to make room for the sawdust factory I was creating on CONTENT, our cat (imaginatively named Kitty) had been showing up less and less frequently—until a few weeks ago, when I realized she had stopped showing up at all. I've seen her around the yard, but she doesn't respond to my greetings and won't even take my phone calls.

It's all part of a pattern of abuse, and I suppose there'll be more in store for me, although it's hard to imagine what could be more of a put-down than to be fired by your cat. Maybe it's me, not the boat. I recall similar incidents from my past, before I owned CONTENT.

I had been sailing in a boat belonging to a friend and had just finished peaking up the gaff (gee, another gaff rig; is there a pattern here?), when a water-skier swooped by and yelled, "Hey, Sinbad!" drenching us both as he deliberately raised a great sheet of water.

I would have cheerfully watched as both driver and skier vanished into a giant whirlpool, but this was in Biscayne Bay, where whirlpools are in woefully short supply. However, it has something even better for Donzi drivers who drive (yes, *drive*) their "boats" while looking astern: shoals. I remember thinking, "Yes, there really is a God," as these cretins drove hard onto one. I sailed serenely past, not even tempted to jeer as I remembered that lovely Spanish adage: Revenge is a dish best eaten cold.

I suppose there is something the gaff rig represents that seems to draw from many people what can best be described as a kind of nostalgic contempt. Folks are glad to see you sail by, but only in the sense that they would be pleased to see someone with a pet raccoon—"Interesting, but thank goodness it's not our raccoon." The implication is, of course, that the geek with the raccoon is either nuts or stupid or both.

The gaff rig is assumed to be an old-fashioned form, good enough in its day, but outmoded today. Now, I'm the first to admit that gaff-rig sailors must be mentally defective in some manner, but that is surely not the fault of the gaff rig. That venerable old rig may attract nuts like me, but to fault the rig for that is like blaming psychosis on the sanitarium. The rig itself is hard to improve upon, although the smug modernist may not realize it.

I do recall a frightful sail one afternoon up in Block Island Sound, when the weather had become quite disgraceful—a rare combination of wind, rain, and fog. CONTENT, as usual, was being passed by everything that floated, although this time our slow speed was due to our having shortened down to a mere wisp of a staysail.

Ordinarily, CONTENT will go like a scalded cat when there's a breeze, but on this day, my good seawife had a roast in the oven and buttermilk biscuits ready to pop in after it. Need I say more about seakindliness? I had shortened sail mainly to avoid lopsided biscuits. Nothing worse on a boat in a bit of weather than lopsided buttermilk biscuits.

I couldn't help but notice that the people aboard the boats passing me were wearing foulweather gear. True, it was raining, but the main problem for them was that they were heeled over so much, they were making a dreadful fuss as they thrashed along. The folks waved as they passed, but they didn't look to me as if they were having much fun. I thought of calling out to one especially white-knuckled skipper that next time he should try going by gaff rig, but then I thought that it probably wasn't the best time for jokes.

I would be less than honest if I did not admit that we got into Block Island hours after the rest of the fleet, but at least we were dry and rested. But, of course, we—like Dangerfield —got "no respect." One of the white-knuckled people called over from his boat, "Glad you made it, finally."

That "finally" nearly got to me. I would have sent him an invitation to join us for dinner just to get even, but I had promised the leftovers to our cat, that ingrate. She had slept all through our passage and was now imperiously demanding dinner.

OK, for you, Kitty; my next pet is going to be a raccoon. Maybe then we'll get some loyalty *and* respect.

CHAPTER 56

Crew Needed: Jolly and Willing

I MADE A BIG mistake the other day. While waiting for some high-tech glop to set up, I strolled over to the boatyard bulletin board to catch up on current events—and succeeded only in having my fragile ego crushed. There were ads by people seeking crew employment and people seeking crew. These ads specified various sailorly skills that I couldn't even spell, let alone understand. And the entire field of nautical knowledge seems to have become infested with acronyms that I don't get. There are people out there, it seems, who are adept at something called SatNav and others who have Trans-Pac experience.

Now, don't get me wrong. I'm not so dumb that I can't figure out that these mouth noises stand for Satellite Navigation and Trans Pacific. I just don't see why a sailor, even a high-tech chap, needs to know how to navigate a satellite or why experience in shipping transmissions across the Pacific has anything to do with qualifications for a good crew. If someone knows the answers to these mysteries, I wish he would keep them to himself.

It's not that I believe high-tech skills are not important, but that far more basic characteristics are much *more* important when it comes to selecting a likely crewmember. Anyone with an operational forebrain can learn nautical skills in a very short time. The smarter the machines are, the dumber we can be. It's infinitely more important for a crewmember to have a non-finicky appetite and a good sense of humor than to be familiar with autopilots or even to know how to steer. Steering can be learned in about 40 seconds, Loran in about an hour; I have seen microwave ovens that require more orientation time than some really sophisticated satellite navigation systems.

No, give me a crewmember who will laugh at my jokes (although some nitwits seem to have difficulty here), eat what's put before him, and come on watch without asking what time it is (it's time for you to come on watch, you moron!), and the question of 100-ton qualifications can be safely ignored. In fact, I wonder—in my rare moments of skepticism—whether there might be an inverse relationship between tonnage licensure and seamanship. I'm thinking of a photograph I saw some time back. It was a photograph of a VLCC (that's the acronym for Very Large Crude Carrier, half a million tons, that is) with a yacht's mast in its anchor flukes. I wonder if anyone had at least said, "Oops!"

Even when technical expertise does happen to be coupled with good, basic seamanship, personality characteristics are more important, because you can't change them. On a long cruise, that fact can be devastating. I once had to spend several days with a chap who had a lovely boat, was an expert seaman, and who knew lots of acronyms. But he also had a habit that made me want to push him overboard: He would reinforce unpleasant circumstances by verbally dwelling on them.

Here's the way it worked: Suppose you had been clawing into half a gale for a day and a half, and you were cold, wet, and tired. "Boy," this twit would say, "I sure am cold, wet, and tired. We've been clawing into this storm for a day and a half." If we were miserable because of wet bunks and fatigue, he would say, "I sure am miserable what with no sleep in the damn wet bunks." I would have murdered him, but it was his boat, a big, heavy ketch, and I didn't know how to work the autopilot.

On the other hand, the best crew I ever sailed with were two middle-aged ladies who had never been on a sailboat before. They adapted immediately to CONTENT's limited living room, made jokes about the cramped quarters, and thought the bad weather that we encountered was just the thing to make their "outing" a grand adventure. Even when frightened, they tried not to show it and went on with their various tasks (my concept of courage).

Naturally, CONTENT's engine failed one morning, and we were forced to break the 60-pound anchor out with the sails. CONTENT's momentum under sail easily broke out the anchor, but my female crew couldn't raise it because their efforts were not synchronized. I became an instant choir master and taught them the words to a short-haul chantey about a gentleman named "Bully John" from Baltimore and his exploits with professional women that involved frequent recourse to the obvious rhyme with that fair city's name.

A quick demonstration of how to pull together with the rhythm of the song was all they needed. My anchor came up so fast that it flew over the roller and almost killed my cat. The ladies were so taken with the song and their newly discovered ability to raise a heavy anchor that for the rest of the cruise they wouldn't let me use the engine or the winch to get the anchor up. They also insisted on learning all the words to the disreputable chantey, and much to my shock and embarrassment, they could not be restrained from singing it in public.

It's a good thing I don't sail in New England anymore, because there are marinas and restaurants from Westport to Nantucket that won't let me in. A great crew, and not a one of them knew a damn thing about sailing (they couldn't carry a tune too well, either), but they were jolly and willing, and I guess that's the point.

CHAPTER 57

From CONTENT to Discontent

AS I GROW older, I am not growing more mellow. Quite the contrary, the list of things that causes me to become poutish and even blasphemous seems to be growing. Where once I hated only jet skis and boats with reverse sheer, I now harbor a litany of peevish irritations. And, don't assume that they are all brought on by modern technology, some of which I heartily approve (such as the serving mallet and the Walker log). No, some aspects of traditional wooden boat sailing have begun to get across my cable.

Take the matter of yawning. I know that people on plastic boats yawn also, but somehow I find a special association between yawning and the navigation of wooden boats. Perhaps it's because, as everyone knows, people who sail wooden boats have a lot more to yawn about. The earliest recollection I have of becoming truly irritated with a fellow sailor's yawning is of a 48-hour period spent rolling at anchor just outside the flats off Bimini. We were engaged in this thankless exercise because the only chart we had was on a placemat from Big Al's Crab Pot, which contained British Admiralty soundings circa 1875, and we were waiting for the weather to clear enough for us to eyeball our way through the reef.

For the week since leaving Miami in a very large and very slow Tahiti ketch, one of our crew could be counted on to do one thing every morning. He would stick his head out of the hatch, slowly glance around the horizon, scratch his belly, and yawn. This yawn would be accompanied by a roar worthy of the MGM lion. It was driving me mad. I refrained from pushing him overboard but, ever since, have been intolerant of loud early-morning yawning under sail—let alone after two days of rolling.

Rolling itself is something I no longer find tolerable. I once accepted it as I accepted yawning, but now I am in favor of abolishing it. No vessel must roll. If one encounters a beam sea, one can change course or even call for air rescue to the nearest Hilton. Not only are beam seas uncomfortable, they make things that are otherwise neutral much worse. Round things, hexagonal things, and worst of all,

155

octagonal things are not inherently sinister, but in a beam sea in the middle of the night they become devices of mental torture.

When a round jelly jar tips over and starts that rhythmic rumble, clunk, rumble, clunk, that's bad enough. But a jar with a polygonal cross section is even worse. It may not roll with each ship's roll, or it may clunk over on only one or two of its faces. The octagonal jar is worst because it probably *will* roll but, like its hexagonal colleague, not the same amount on each of the vessel's rolls. That sets the unhappy mariner up for the most alarming question the sailor can ask or think in the middle of the night. I'm sure you know what that question is, but just for the record, it's "What the hell was that?" That single question has been responsible for more adrenaline secretion than all Super Bowl Sundays combined, and the trauma to the floorboards cannot be calculated.

And, what about those floorboards? (I've given up calling them "cabin soles," but that's another column.) I have a favorite fantasy, and it goes like this: Every yacht designer who draws or actually specifies on the materials list those conventional floorboards that form a solid and continuous expanse of wood, composite goop, or even good old cork (I said it was a fantasy) that is supposedly removable by those little brass rings, should be forced to find the damn ring and remove the section of flooring at 0300 hours with all the interior lights kaput. And he should be forced to do this while the sound of gurgling water is reminding him that he is mortal.

Even when he finds the ring, it should be jammed in place by years of impacted grunge. If he manages to free it at last, he will find that he can only get one finger through it and that exerting more than six pounds of pull raises a practical question of how much pain and blood loss can be endured, mortal terror notwithstanding.

If I ever reach the point in my work on CONTENT where I am ready to make new floor boards, they will be boards— big ones with big holes in them. And they will *not* fit tightly to their neighbors. They will not look like the dance floor of a disco, and a dropped fork might fall through to the bilge. But I will be able to pick up various sections quite easily, even when terrified. And I might leave extra-large spaces in the galley so that, with luck, jars with octagonal cross sections can fall into the bilge and let me get back to sleep.

CHAPTER 58

Tides of Change

OR SOME TIME, I have suspected that things in the maritime world have been changing without anyone having had the decency to consult me. I didn't object when they stopped using seconds of arc in navigational tables and switched to decimal minutes. I didn't object when the Coast Guard stopped training signal personnel in Morse Code. I have even gotten used to the fact that boatyards smell more like high school chemistry labs than wood shops. I accept all of this; I'm no Neanderthal. But some of the eternal verities have begun to change, and now, I'm sorry to say, I must put my foot down.

When for instance, waxed line for whipping the ends of rope has given way to little plastic sleeves that shrink tight when heated with a match, something has been lost. It's not that those gimmicks don't work as well as hand whipping. My objection is that they work as well or better. You can't separate skilled from the unskilled anymore. Anyone can light a match. You can no longer have idiotic arguments with other sailors over the best of the dozens of methods of whipping a line. Those damned plastic sleeves seem to hold forever and never slip.

But I resist the tide of change. CONTENT's lines are still whipped by the so-called "sailmaker's whipping." In addition, CONTENT's lines show some personal uniqueness, some individuality. This is due to my never having correctly mastered the sailmaker's whipping. I end up with something that *looks* just like sailmaker's whipping but after a few weeks one of those pretty little wraps that go around the outside of the main layer of wraps comes loose. So, you can tell one of CONTENT's whipped lines from all the rest because those three pretty little outside wraps have become two, plus a fetching little tail of waxed line waving in the breeze. It may be a lousy whipping but, by Godfrey, it's *my* lousy whipping. If you had used a heat-shrink sleeve and somehow gotten it wrong (although how anyone could get one wrong is hard to imagine) and the sleeve had, say, shrunk unevenly, it would also be a lousy job, but it would have been a plastic company's lousy job. See my point? The personality has been removed from the matter.

Another eternal verity concerning line is that one should not cleat a line by finishing with a hitch. Nowadays, plastic braided line has turned that rule on its head. These lines are slippery as eels and if you *don't* finish with a hitch, they're likely to slither off the cleat. I have a firm rule on CONTENT that has worked so far to resist this tide of change. That rule is: No braided line aboard that has not been fished out of the boatyard dumpster. Wondering why it was thrown away in the first place, I am never tempted to use the salvaged line for anything really critical.

"Log, line, and lookout" once was the old salt's eternal verity for keeping his vessel off the beach. I once thought I was being oh-so-open-minded when I learned to use Loran. It seemed decadent to know one's position without having to *work* for it. I felt like asking my H.O. 229 Sight Reduction Tables for forgiveness. Lately, however, I have been made aware that even the simplicity of Loran has been simplified. There are satellite navigation computers that just flat-out give you your position. I'm not sure, but I believe that all you have to do is *wish* to know it. I don't know how that works, but I think you have to close your eyes and tap your little red shoes together three times.

I suppose it's narrow-minded of me to lament the "progress" happening all around me, especially when I am among the beneficiaries of that progress. But doing sailorly tasks in a half-assed manner is sometimes more satisfying than having, say, DuPont or NOAA do them for you, however perfectly.

I like the feeling that no one else whips a line wrong exactly the way I do it wrong. Even if the whipping comes undone, there's no harm. I have these nifty little heat-shrink things in place an inch or so away from the traditional whipping, just in case. Wearing a belt doesn't mean you can't also wear suspenders.

CHAPTER 59

When Function Follows Form

I HAVE A CONFESSION. I have been "on the beach" so long I fear I may have lost some of my nautical skills. Oh, I know one never forgets the basic stuff, like how to quickly discover where the 220-volt outlets are or where in the pluperfect hell the marina management hides the dock carts. I'm referring to skills one develops after many years of living aboard one particular boat.

After several years of living ashore in something called a house (you know, where you can stand up straight even when you're inside), I am no longer certain that I can slither through the main cabin in one step, hip-wiggling to avoid the cabin table while simultaneously ducking my head to avoid the skylight jacks, arriving in the galley just in time to jerk the dead lizard out of my cat's mouth before she can drop it into the bilge. I have been told that cats do this sort of thing because they like you and just want to bring you a "present." The truth be known, I'd just as soon have a gift certificate from Sears.

After years aboard CONTENT, every step, shoulder twitch, head duck, handhold, from every point to every other point, from masthead to keel, had become an automatic and deft, well-choreographed routine. After many years ashore, however, I may have suffered some atrophy of those skills. The other day, as I moved rapidly forward into the galley to search out the latest leak, I whacked my head on a skylight jack handle. That had not happened in years. I had become so confident that I had long since removed the woolen socks that had been wrapped around it. But I had forgotten that to get from the main cabin into the galley the routine was step, twist, duck, step; and so I performed the routine as step, twist, thunk . . . "dammit!" step. Not only did I not find the leak (heck, I barely found the galley), but now I duck even when there's no need to. I have some pride, though: I will not, and I mean I will not, rewrap the offending hardware with old woolen socks. After first developing a high tolerance for skull pain, I know that I shall eventually regain my flawless ducking form.

Now, the galley itself is the venue of certain delicate skills that can easily atrophy through inactivity. I'm not referring to cooking skills. Heck, anyone who can read can cook. I'm talking about fine art now. For instance, one of my secret delights was in being able to light the diesel stove with one match. After all these years, can I still do that?

Don't laugh. I care deeply about this and it isn't easy. First, the alcohol primer is poured into the primer cup and ignited. Then, at the precise moment that the alcohol flame is about to go out but is still big enough to pass by the ports in the burner, you turn the burner valve on. If your timing has been exquisite, the diesel vapor will ignite with a clean blue flame just as the yellow-blue flame of the alcohol goes out. Anyone who can't feel the intense satisfaction of that is probably one of that oafish clan who can eat an Oreo cookie without first splitting it in half with his front teeth.

Now, assuming that the burner has been properly ignited and CONTENT-style coffee brewed, can I still drink it properly? CONTENT-style coffee has most of the physical characteristics of pine tar, although my good seawife says it doesn't taste as good. Properly drinking it means that one never appears hurried, no matter what might be going on.

I believe that drinking hot coffee slowly, out of a china cup *with saucer*, no matter the nature of the crisis, constitutes the epitome of nautical panache. For instance, suppose you're approaching the dock under power and the inevitable instructions have begun to bellow forth from the inevitable instructors on the pier. Do you bellow back? You do not. You sip. Pause. Sip again. If you are forced to actually do something, you put down your coffee as slowly as your nerves and the situation will allow and do what is needed as slowly as possible. Bear in mind that it's better to allow a minor mishap to occur than to admit by hurrying that you've miscalculated. That may seem an incorrect order of priorities, but not to us wooden boat sailors. We know that when it comes to a choice of outward appearance versus real substance, outward appearance wins, hands down.

CHAPTER 60

The Bigger, the Better

NOBODY ASKED ME, but I'll tell you anyway: Marine stuff doesn't work as well as land stuff because marine stuff is typically just a toy version of the corresponding land stuff. Take a look at the galley of a modern yacht. The sink is a toy sink, barely one-third the size of a real grown-up sink. The oven, in the unlikely event there is one, is too small for cooking anything larger than a hummingbird. That may be appropriate for a cleanup task that must be accomplished in a sink the size of a music box, but I worry about a diet too rich in hummingbirds (those tiny bones, you know?), and the ranges, those little alcohol ranges that produce no practical amount of heat, are a snare and a delusion. The studious mariner can use his time while waiting for coffee water to boil on such a range by acquiring a good basic grasp of conversational Bulgarian.

Even the layout of the modern yacht is based on the toy motif. The saloon ("salon" is a modernism based on a mistake, but more on that in a future monograph) is a perfect example. Originally, the word referred to any large ornate room intended for formal entertaining. The word went to sea on passenger liners and large wooden schooner-yachts sailed in New England by men in white ducks who knew their brandy and had mastered the craft of talking without moving their jaws. Some of these men may still be observed, but their habitat has shrunk to the New York Yacht Club and a handful of quiet old-money preserves along the New England littoral. I suspect that the survivors have been propelled—by the savings and loan disaster—down the path of the passenger pigeon and greater auk.

What an irony that a word that once stood for crystal chandeliers and fine stemware now is applied to an area only somewhat larger than that of a doll's house. Table, seats, fixtures all suggest toys. And anyone who has ever tried to cook and serve dinner for four or (God forbid!) six in one of these doll's houses knows that the feat, even when brought off, has more to do with playing skillfully with toys than behaving like a grown-up. The only way that two people can sit side-by-side in a typical "salon" is for them to

remember how much fun it was when they were children and gig-
gling side-by-side in a shipping carton.

Sad to say, if you want a grown-up version of a nautical thing
such as a sink or stove or table, you'll have to go where the grown-
ups go: a hardware store or builder's supply store or restaurant supply outlet. Stay away from toy stores—i.e., marine stores. We found
this out when we were looking for galley equipment for old CON-
TENT. My good seawife, who had had plenty of cruising experience,
disdained all the sinks we could find in marine stores. "Too damn
shallow," she would say. "I don't want a soaking with dishwater
every time the boat heels. I want a deep sink!" We finally found a
very un-marine-looking, deep, double stainless-steel sink in a
friendly restaurant suppliers' warehouse.

And now, dear friends, a word about gimbals, both for stoves and
sinks: No. Great idea on paper, but out there in the real, wet, and im-
perfect world, they don't work—not on small boats, they don't. They
never have enough swinging room, for one thing: So, instead of tipping
gradually and spilling a dollop of Hormel's glop as the boat heels, they
don't tip at all until WHAM! they slam up against the inside of the hull
and propel pot contents all over the place. Please don't tell me that the
gimbals can always be locked. No, they can't. You used to be able to
lock the damned stove gimbals, but now the little knurled knob that
drives the set-screw cannot be found. If found, it will be discovered that
the set-screw has long since scribed a deep arc in the side of the stove.
Naturally, some nitwit, probably you, has habitually failed to tighten it
down sufficiently, allowing this bit of unwanted engraving to occur. In
harbor, when one does not want or need a gimbaled anything, count-
less pots of coffee are capsized by unwitting folks, probably you again,
who cannot seem to remember either to place coffee pots above the precisely calculated center of mass of the stove or to jam a winch handle
right . . . there . . . so that the stove will stay put. Again, the best seagoing stove is a stove that might be found in a house; you know, a
grown-up stove that has four legs and sits on the floor (OK, OK, the
cabin sole) and burns something that actually makes things hot.

That means almost any hydrocarbon from coal to buffalo dung,
excluding alcohol, of course. Alcohol stoves are not merely toys;
they are dangerous toys, made even more so by the curious canard
that has somehow gotten about that alcohol is safer than other fuels.
I do not think it is safer than diesel. Maybe it's safer than naphtha,
but I suppose the last naphtha launch blew up years ago.

Dining tables on yachts (even the teak one on CONTENT) are really toy tables, pale imitations of the real shoreside article. A schooner skipper of my acquaintance had the best table aboard a boat that I have ever seen: a folding bridge table that he purchased at K-Mart. He would set it up in his cockpit, spread a table cloth, set out his china and silverware, and entertain his friends just like grown-ups.

On CONTENT, we are much more nautical, crammed in and hunched over our postage-stamp-sized beautiful teak table—you know, the one with the damn gimbals. Sailing, you are afraid to touch the table because it might interfere with its swing. In harbor, someone (I'm not mentioning names) will forget to lock the gimbals and then rest his elbows on it or set a heavy pot upon it. Now I lock the thing with a pair of C-clamps, but I know what I really need is a folding bridge table. I wonder if K-Mart has one that would be right for an old English cutter.

CHAPTER 61

American Practical Naviguesser

T HERE IS SO much claptrap written about the navigation of sailing vessels that I would like to take this opportunity to contribute to it. Navigation is like just about everything else: There are more ways to do it wrong than to do it right. And that goes in spades for deep-draft old wooden boats, I can tell you. For these craft, even things that are right can be wrong a good part of the time.

A certain skipper (I forbear to mention names) became confused in one of those awful New England fogs. (OK . . . , it was me, and I wasn't confused; I just didn't know whether I was off Rhode Island or Massachusetts.) So I did what you're not supposed to do. I followed someone who looked as if he knew what he was doing—a tug pulling a deeply laden barge. He has plenty of draft, thought I. If he can go there, I can go there. This looked to me like one of those times when what is generally wrong might actually be right. Wrong. Soon, the tug, the barge, and I, went crunch, in that order.

"Damn fool," I thought. "I'm new to this neck of the woods, but this guy should have known better." Four hours later, when I was vertical while lying on deck, the tug skipper cleared up my lack of comprehension. Through the bullhorn, he said (his voice trembling with the effort not to laugh), "I see you've come to dig shale, too, eh Cap?"

I still think the admonition not to follow someone else when you're nautically "challenged" is not necessarily correct, but in the future I shall try to raise my intended guide on Channel 16 and question him closely as to his mission.

Non-standard methods of navigation can be much more reliable than going by the book. I have often wondered why so-called navigational aids are so damned hard to find compared to things like chimneys and water towers. Height alone doesn't explain it, for many lighthouses are plenty tall. However, I've never seen a lighthouse as easy to pick out at night as your garden variety Buick dealer; I believe that the folks who design navigational aids deliberately make matters difficult in order to maintain the panache of sailing. If it were made too easy, heck, anyone could do it. As a matter of fact, lots more people could do it if they would just learn to use non-nautical sources of data.

As in the case of my following the tug, even relying on such quasi-nautical aids as land structures has its pitfalls. Church steeples, for instance, may be noted on the chart, but watch out—things are never as simple as they seem.

I was once approaching Montauk Point under conditions of reduced competence when I spied a church steeple where there should not have been one. I luffed up and dove frantically into my chart. No, I should not have been seeing church steeples. Yes, there is Montauk Light, and what in the pluperfect hell is going on here?!

What was going on was a tug pulling a barge upon which was a church steeple—no church, just the steeple. I am sure that the S.O.B. with the gravel barge must moonlight as a church steeple transporter. I am upset that there is no day or night signal for "I am towing a church steeple." I shall never get over the feeling that some part of Montauk containing a church had broken loose and floated out into the eastern reaches of Long Island Sound.

Certainly there is historical precedent for parts of New England coming adrift. A certain old Nantucket schooner captain was in the habit of tasting the sediment brought up by the leadsman as they were returning from the Grand Banks. Savoring the bottom like a gourmet passing judgment on his truffles, he would spit and call out a course for home. (An English sea captain once made a habit of biting down on the bits of gravel that he recovered from the tallow of his deep-sea lead. When a journalist visitor asked him why, he said, "If I can bust 'em, we be east of Dogger Banks, otherwise we be west.")

At the start of one voyage, the Nantucket skipper's crew decided to play a prank on the old man and to see whether there was anything in this strange gustatory navigational tactic. Before departure, the mate hid a bit of Nantucket soil in his seabag, and when the lead was recovered on the vessel's return, he slyly pressed a bit of the soil into the tallow before handing it to the skipper. The skipper tasted it, wrinkled his brow, and called out to the crew, "Say your prayers, lads, for Nantucket has sunk and we be right over Ma Nickerson's henyard!"

Whether you believe this story or not, my sermon amounts to this: There are more weird ways to navigate than are dreamt of in *Bowditch*.

CHAPTER 62

Stuff We Don't Know

I HEAR THAT LOTS of folks, even sailors of wooden boats, are becoming more and more technologically sophisticated. Baloney, I say. That statement is just the latest in my ever-growing collection called *stuff what folks know is so but what ain't*. Engineers and scientists are becoming more and more technologically sophisticated, but the rest of us poor schnooks are standing around saying, "Jeez."

Sure, electronic bric-a-brac can be found on lots of small boats these days, but not many of us know how the things work. If I buy a computerized navigation thingy for my MARIE CELESTE replica, even assuming the dubious proposition that I learn which buttons to push, I haven't become more sophisticated. Poorer, yes; sophisticated, no. In fact, I have become *less* sophisticated in the ratio of what I do know relative to what I *should* know if I knew everything there was to know . . . if you know what I mean.

OK, I can see that I'm going too fast for some of you in the back. Look: Suppose that I've finally learned how to get a fix by two intersecting celestial LOPs via sextant, almanac, and reduction tables. However, while I've been learning this, the latest marine show has exhibited a black box that you just turn on and ask, "Where in GOD's name am I?!" and the black box tells you. (Actually, you don't even have to turn it on, because it's voice activated.) I've gained enough knowledge to catch up with the average skipper of the late 19th century, but technology has surged into the early 21st. If you bend on a little jib tops'l while your opponent bends on a spinnaker, he'll be finishing up the last of the watery flat punch in the clubhouse while you're still blowing the horn for the launch.

Even in such a traditional matter as old-fashioned celestial navigation, we are less sophisticated than ever. That 19th-century skipper had to know spherical trigonometry in order to solve the navigational triangle. No sight reduction tables for him. Could you do that? I didn't think so. And those degrees and minutes in the sight reduction tables . . . how did they get there? Who figured out all that stuff? I'm sure there are plenty of people who know, but I'm not one of them, and neither, I suspect, are you. We're a bunch of schnooks. We can use sight reduction tables because someone told us how to, but most of us don't know what's behind them. By contrast, old Cap'n Stormalong in the 19th century understood spherical trigonometry because back then, you just couldn't use that stuff unless you understood it. Any schnook can "enter" the tables at the right page and find the intersection of column this and line that and come up with a thing called Hc. And even given this, many people can't work an LOP unless they have a pre-printed "worksheet" to tell them where to put the numbers. It reminds me of the related disability of being unable to reconcile your checkbook balance with the bank statement unless you slavishly follow the format printed on the back of the statement. I know all about that, because I am one of those people.

So, not only have we fallen behind in a relative sense due to advancing technology, we have even fallen behind in an absolute sense. We know even less than the average 19th-century poor schnook.

I recall seeing a photocopy of the front page of a New York newspaper from about 1860. The lead story described a new clipper being launched at a Manhattan yard. This story, written for the general reader, mind you, described the hull in terms of "half-breadths," "waterlines," "entry," "run aft," etc. Obviously, folks back then knew more about their technology than we know about ours, and most of us have forgotten much of their technology in the bargain. It's not bad enough that we don't know how satellite navigation really works, but we also don't remember (if we ever knew) what a serving mallet is and how to use one.

I think it's important to keep our egos under control in this matter, to remember that not only have we not gotten any smarter, we really haven't gotten any more sophisticated. We know which buttons to push, but we really don't know what the hell happens after that, except that we get the right answer . . . mostly.

And when we don't? Do we fix the gizmo? Of course we don't fix it. We haven't the foggiest idea how it works. We send for Al, the nerd with the plastic pen holder in his shirt pocket. Al doesn't really know how the gizmo works, either, but he can sometimes narrow the trouble down to the veeblefetzer unit. Neither does he know how the veeblefetzer unit works, but he can get another one in six weeks.

Does anyone know how to actually repair anything anymore? Good grief . . . no one knows how anything works anymore. Don't believe me? The next time Al comes out to your boat to scratch his head over your gizmo, see what kind of response you get (after he tells you he'll have to send the gizmo back to Singapore for "recalibration") when you ask him to take a look at your busted serving mallet.

CHAPTER 63

It's Just Common Scents

TO GO BELOW decks in CONTENT is to realize the importance of the nose as a source of data about the outside world. You can't hear much, because her wooden hull is a good sound insulator, and all you can see is sky because she has no portholes. But you can smell all sorts of interesting things—once you get past the scent of CONTENT herself, which is a heavy blend of diesel, tar, oakum, and chronic indebtedness.

Here's a hypothetical case that illustrates my olfactory theory: You're below in CONTENT, seemingly cut off from the outside world except for the distant hum of the Travel-Lift and a patch of sky visible through the open skylight. Suddenly you smell gasoline engine exhaust, suntan glop, light machine oil, hickory smoke (or a reasonable facsimile), burning mammalian fat, more gasoline exhaust, mustard—all roughly in that order.

The single explanation for this particular sequence of these particular smells is abundantly clear to the experienced nose. The gasoline-engine exhaust's *sudden* olfactory onset means that the modern fiberglass yacht next to you has just fired up his engine. Why modern fiberglass? Simple. If it were an old wooden boat, the engine would probably be diesel, and if it should happen to be gasoline, the damn thing wouldn't run because there would just *have* to be something wrong with it; probably something pretty serious, such as having been built in England.

Suntan glop means young people in bathing suits, probably tourists. People who sail old wooden boats never wear bathing suits or use suntan glop. Also, they are never young. Even if they were young when they took to wooden boats, they aged fast.

The light machine oil is, of course, "starter" for the charcoal. And that immediately explains the fake hickory smoke, and from these facts we may infer a hibachi, a Japanese device for inflating everybody's insurance premiums, especially when used in conjunction with gasoline engines and charcoal. In fact, I would here interject a little hint to the prudent mariner: Anything that suggests the presence of a hibachi aboard a neighboring boat should cause one to immediately check that the little pointer on the fire extinguisher is in the green arc. If you're downwind, remove the extinguisher from the retaining clips.

The odor of burning fat is, of course, either due to the cooking going on, or someone having ignited himself. In the latter case, I would suggest that you promptly close the skylights. Finally—and this is very tricky—the smell of exhaust fumes followed by the odor of mustard means that someone forgot the essential condiment, drove to the grocery store, and returned—a culinary hero.

Be forewarned that the preceding sequence of smells is often followed by a related syndrome: fiberglass repairs that start very early in the morning to the accompaniment of radio music performed by singers and instrumentalists who always seem very angry about something. Strictly speaking, one may point out that music is an aural and not an olfactory phenomenon. But, as a longtime sufferer, I would counter that such is not the case.

The fiberglass repairs are easy to identify by nose alone. When you smell aromas that are normally associated with Secaucus. New Jersey, you know that someone is repairing his plastic boat. Naturally, this tip does not apply if you are actually in Secaucus, in which case, my condolences.

The nose can be a great help when one is sailing. For instance, the time I was almost run down by the TOYOTA MARU in New York's Ambrose Channel, my first warning was the smell of bacon and coffee coming from a direction in which bacon and coffee were not supposed to be. And I can recall one night in thick weather on Long Island Sound when I was able to catch the distinct aroma of pine woods. Pleasant as that aroma is, it is quite out of place when you think you are several miles offshore. On the night in question, moments after smelling the woods I found I was able to take a most pleasant walk in them simply by jumping off the end of CONTENT's bowsprit.